I.C.E.: Eye See Everything
The True Life of Kendrick Watson

All Facts ~ No Fiction

By Kendrick Watson

Powder Springs, GA

Published in Powder Springs, Georgia by J&C Legacy
Publishing.

Printed in the United States of America

 ISBN: 978-0-578-90367-5

Disclaimer

The purpose of this book is to share, encourage, and enlighten the reader to the injustices within our justice system.

I have tried to recreate events, locales, and conversations from my memories of them. I have added supporting documentation where needed and able. In order to maintain their anonymity in some instances I have changed the names of individuals and places, I may have changed some identifying characteristics and details such as physical properties, occupations, and places of residence.

Although the author and publisher have made every effort to ensure that the information in this book was correct at press time, the author and publisher do not assume and hereby disclaim any liability to any party for any loss, damage, or disruption caused by errors or omissions, whether such errors or omissions result from negligence, accident, or any other cause.

The author and publishing company shall have neither liability nor responsibility to any person or entity with respect to any loss or damage caused, or alleged to have been caused, directly or indirectly, by the information contained in this book.

If you do not wish to be bound by the above, you may return this book to the publisher for a full refund.

Rest In Peace
Humphrie' C. Ford

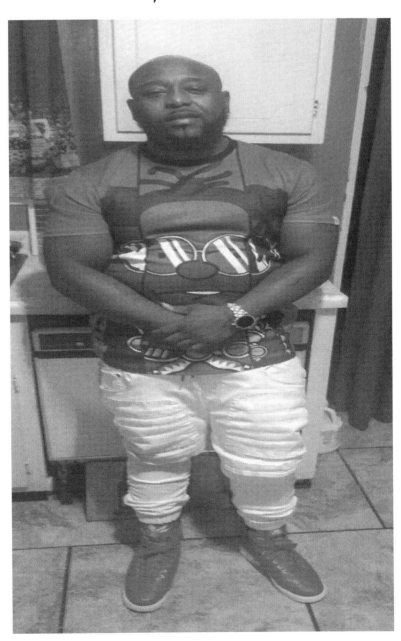

This book is dedicated to those who were served injustice or locked up illegally.

I am speaking on your behalf.

Acknowledgements

First, I would like to give all thanks and glory to God.

To my mother, Dewise A. Watson, Sister, Celitria Watson, my best friend in the world, April Malone, my kids Torey, Corey, Kendarius, Traven, Demario, Acasia, and Kourtland.

To all my friends who road with me in this struggle, Wycel, Dex, Moe Muji, Rodney Jenkins, Michelle, Black Rico, Van Rico, Jeremy Alexander, Eddie Hodges, Ronald Hudson, Jamaal, Mia, James Clark, Voodoo the Priest, Sherman Lewis, Wild D, and Travis Mathews.

To all my co-defendants that kept it real with me, Lil' Stew, Drama, Theo, Uncle Bubba, Gino, Lil' Larry Barnes, and Big Nose.

I want to give a special thanks to Ms. Sharon Rondeau at The Post and email for writing articles on my case once the facts was presented to her. Thanks to Paul Springer, Terrell Tooten, and last but not least, thanks to the corrupt law enforcement agents Therman Richardson, Johnathan Overly, and William Acred, without y'all I wouldn't have got the opportunity to expose more corrupt prosecutors and judges that's effecting the justice system.

I would like to thank Trevino Campbell, LaMario Porter, Larry Fung, Ernest Butter, Wendell King, and Rico Collins. I appreciate ya'll for listening to me complain and express my concerns about my case over the years, and I can't forget my Editor, Chanelle Watson. Thanks for doing an amazing job on bringing my writing on my life to reality. I know the readers are going to enjoy going on this journey of exploring the fine prints of I.C.E.

"The ultimate measure of a man is not where he stands in moments of comfort and convenience, but where he stands at times of challenge and controversy."

~ Rev. Dr. Martin Luther King, Jr.

I.C.E.: Eye See Everything
The True Life of Kendrick Watson

All Facts ~ No Fiction

Table of Contents

Judicial & Frequently Used Terms & Abbreviations

Here are some judicial phrases and frequently used abbreviations and terms that I will be using occasionally in the book. Please keep them in mind as you take this journey with me through my life experiences. The terms are defined as I understand and use them:

C.C.A. – Corrections Corporation of America

F.C.I. – Federal Correctional Institution

U.S.P. – United States Penitentiary

Backpage – an on-line site used to traffic sexual acts (prostitution) and under illegal products and services

"Sunshine State" – The state of California

L.M.G – LeMoyne Garden is a public housing project in South Memphis, TN

Sting Ray Device – cellular phone surveillance device used by the police to tap cell phones

F.B.I. (Feds) – Federal Bureau of Investigation

A.T.F. – governmental agency that deals specifically with Alcohol, Tobacco, Fire Arms

P.S.I. – Pre-Sentence Investigator

Snitch – an informant or someone who exposes the illegal

acts of another person to the police

G.E.D. – General Equivalency Development Certificate, shows that you have a level of knowledge equivalent to a high school graduate

Unicor - Federal Prison Industries (commonly referred to as FPI, or by its trade name UNICOR), is a wholly-owned government corporation established by Congress on June 23, 1934. Its mission is to protect society and reduce crime by preparing inmates for successful reentry through job training.

Compound – the area in the prison where the inmates would come together

C.O. – Correctional Officer(s)

S.I.S. – Security Investigations Specialists

P.O. – Parole Officer (s)

Connect – individual who sells drugs or an illegal substance

Middleman – the person who is the link between the Connect and the person who wants to sell the illegal substance

Aquarius

Aquarius: the sign of the future and the visionary. Aquarians are unorthodox, original people – sort of wacky, who refuse to follow the crowd, and go their own way. Aquarians LIKE being different. They not only march to a different drummer, they make up new music as they go along.

Intellectual independence is the most marked characteristic. Their personality is liberal, progressive, yet fixed in opinion. Their inflexibility shows up when others least expect it. It may be in defense of an idea, a trip decided on, a habit they refuse to give up – whatever the cause, sometimes people will suddenly realize the Aquarian obstinacy. With women, Aquarian men sometimes refuse to compromise or give an inch.

Aquarians cheerfully ignore what the critics think and strike off on new paths, unbound by opinions, because there are so many more exciting things for them to discover that way. They hate boredom and take every opportunity to avoid it.

The Aquarian character is a system of paradoxes. They enjoy being with people but are content to be alone. They like to travel but love relaxing at home. Aquarians are friendly and outgoing but also detached and reserved. They have both a scientific and artistic mind.

Aquarians are communicators, idea people. People born under this sign live most intensely in their minds. This sign stands for truth. They are truth-tellers. They give out opinions and observations. They dispense wisdom. Aquarians are seekers of knowledge, rational, open-minded, and gifted - with breadth of vision. Chock full of information, they still search for more. Aquarians always want to know what's on the either side of the mountain. One Aquarian said, "It annoys me to find out there's something out there I've never heard of. I need to know what it is!"

They don't let emotions get in the way of their judgments. This appears to give them the ability to stand outside of themselves, to rise above ordinary human weaknesses. Aquarians don't trust emotions.

Aquarians are very people-oriented, addicted to the stud of human beings, and are people-watchers. They are outgoing and attract friends wherever they go. Aquarians have a talent for making people laugh. Those who decide to tangle with them quickly find out that their sharp verbal skills can quickly deflate a big head. Whoever they meet, Aquarians remain themselves – that amusing, inquisitive, interested person who wants to know what makes others tick. Their gift is for dealing with all kinds of personalities from every walk of life, no matter what the station or status. Aquarians never put on airs. If they met the Queen of England, they would be their natural self. They are generally interested in why a person thinks the way they do. The nicest part is that they do not judge. Aquarians willingly grant to others what they consider to be a natural right, the freedom to be different. For them, the ultimate liberation is simply the freedom to be oneself.

Because independence is the Aquarian way of life, they will sacrifice even a close personal relationship in order to maintain it. Trying to fence them in or tie them down won't work. If an Aquarian feels trapped, they try to break free at any cost. The sign of Aquarius also represents future hopes; for them, what is over, is done. They want to escape the past. Aquarians are wonderful at hatching schemes and dreams, plotting trips, setting goals. The unusual – in people, places, and projects – is what really interests them.

As an idealist, the Aquarian would like to see that everybody is happy, and his or her ambition is to do something important and meaningful. Many Aquarians go into politics or get involved in social causes.

An Aquarian will hatch up a grandiose scheme for improving the way things are, but their main interest is in creating the idea, not translating it into action. Hard work doesn't interest an Aquarian. They are creative, imaginative, endlessly willing to experiment, but getting caught up in the small details is not their style. They'd much rather employ others to handle that.

Aquarians are so determined not to be like anyone else they are sometimes contrary, just to be different. Sometimes they will be argumentative not because they feel deeply, but simply because they enjoy intellectual exercise.

Nevertheless, Aquarians are among the kindest people in the world. Easygoing, reasonable, slow to take offense, never mean-hearted, they believe in live – and – let – live. Honest, helpful, and best of all never boring, Aquarians can change anyone's life for the better, just by becoming part of it.

The Inner Aquarian

The most frequent question Aquarians ask is "Why?" They want to understand what makes people tick. The lives of others fascinate Aquarians because they hope they will offer insights into their own. Aquarians have plenty of love to give, and want nothing more than to have lots of interesting friends, a wonderful love relationship, fulfilling work, for the world to be a better place, and everyone to be happy. Not much to ask, is it? One of their best kept secrets is how shy and insecure they are. They wonder if the people they care about feel the same way about them. Yet somehow their feelings of insecurity manage to coexist with a belief that they are someone special.

How Others See Aquarians

Aquarians are often regarded as slightly eccentric – not necessarily strange, but certainly an independent character, a kind of daredevil with an unusual way of looking at things. People are drawn to their friendliness and enthusiasm, but withdraw quickly when they become acid-tongued. Sometimes, because they need so much personal freedom, Aquarians give the impression of being uncaring or distant. Those around them may also become annoyed at their stubbornness.

Me... I.C.E. is this Aquarian.

I.C.E.: Eye See Everything
The True Life of Kendrick Watson

All Facts ~ No Fiction

1

First Things First: Let Me Introduce Myself

Hello world, allow me to introduce myself. My real name is Kendrick Watson, but my family and associates call me Jerry. I was born in January 1980 in Mabayou, Mississippi. But, my mother, father, sister, and I lived in the small town of Rosedale, Mississippi. When I was five years old, my parents separated which caused my sister and me to be raised by our mother in a single parent home.

My mother did the best she could to provide us with the necessary bare essentials and to make-ends-meet. She worked various small jobs like chopping cotton, during the spring and summer seasons, or babysitting and housecleaning for the more upper class citizens. She was so dedicated to keeping a roof over our heads that she would sometimes allow our house to be used for prostitution. Her girlfriends would come over and entertain older guys for money. I guess they were the type of men who weren't getting the kind of gratification they wanted at home, so they would step out on their wives. Me and my sister's bedroom would be used to satisfy their long, neglected, sexual passions, and desires by sleeping with these strange women.

Mom did her best to shield me and my sister's eyes from these illicit activities going on in our home by sending us next door to be babysat by our neighbor. But after our babysitter went to sleep, we would sneak out of the house and peek through the windows of our home in order to alleviate our young and curious minds.

Now my father, on the other hand, eventually decided to spread his wings and moved to Massachusetts to work on a ship that paid good money. I always stayed in touch with his side of the family by always visiting my grandparents. My grandfather was a preacher and a well-respected figure. My grandmother, the first lady of the church, was always the centerpiece of our large family. She consistently kept everyone involved in Church from Monday through Sunday and she NEVER missed preparing a big Sunday feast. Their house was the gathering spot after Church was over and all the grandchildren came over to eat and play.

My cousins Patrick, Jawaskii, and I were very close. They are my older cousins and by the time I was seven years old, we were completely inseparable. I would always find a way to spend the night at their house, especially on the weekends.

Jawaskii was the oldest out of us three and was the most active and competitive. He would always find ways to set-up backyard fights where Patrick and I would fight other neighborhood kids whom we had just finished playing with minutes before. I never saw Jawaskii himself fight anyone but he would occasionally compete in ground gymnastic activities that he organized for us kids.

There was a close friend of mine, who I'll call, Roderick. He had a pretty big family who I got along with just fine. They loved to go hunting and did so every night for the food they planned to eat. They hunted deer, rabbit, raccoons, etc. I really admired the way they stayed close together as a family.

Occasionally, I would spend nights at Roderick's

family's house and not just for the food either. Roderick had a sister, who I'll call, Gwen that I could not keep my hands off of. After everyone was asleep at night Gwen and I would play the "touchie-touchie-feelie-feelie" game. We used to kiss one another all night. I never really understood those times when my mom's friends would come over, especially after my encounters with Gwen because just kissing all night didn't seem that amazing.

But, all of that changed when we moved in with my mother's father Ned. Ned would always confine us to one room or send us outside to play whenever my mom sent us over his house to be babysat. He used to always sit in his favorite recliner chair with a fan blowing and watch these weird V.C.R. tapes. I would soon learn later in life they are called XXX-rated movies.

One day while we were outside playing I called out to my grandfather to alert him that I was coming inside the house to use the bathroom. He didn't answer, so, I walked into the house unannounced and witnessed a pornographic scene on the television that my eyes were too young to see. My grandfather had fallen asleep and left the V.C.R. on. What I saw that day changed my life forever. I was officially ready to show Gwen something a little different the next time I spent a night at her house. And when I did, boy did we enjoy our first sexual experience at the tender age of eight.

2

The Move to Memphis

Throughout my childhood my mother would periodically travel back and forth from Rosedale to Memphis, Tennessee. A couple of times we even tried moving to Memphis for good. But, for some reason we would always find our way back to Rosedale.

Mom met a guy named Joe Lee. He was always good to her and I remember them always being happy together. At first, I didn't want to accept him as a father figure, but he eventually won my young heart over. He took a lot of time out with me and plus, he had some younger siblings, and some nieces and nephews that were close enough to me and my sister's age for us to play with.

Joe Lee's consistent work ethics inspired me and made me want to get a job also. Since I was too young to get a real job, I would go out and fill up garbage bags with pecans, alongside with the other children and some adults. At the end of the day I would have enough money to buy all of the candy that my young teeth could handle.

One year, around the spring season, Joe Lee and my mother finally decided that they'd had enough of Mississippi. We were finally ready to relocate. So, Joe Lee stole some checks from his workplace and we packed up and moved to Memphis, permanently. My sister and I were enrolled into Grandview Elementary School. We moved into my great aunt's house, who I'll call, Tee. She allowed us to live with her until my mother was able to find a job, get on her feet, and find a place of her own.

Not long after our move, the crimes that Joe Lee had committed back in Mississippi came back to haunt him. One day while we were getting ready for school there was a banging on Tee's door. It was the Shelby County Sheriff's department with a warrant for Joe Lee's arrest. He went along without any hassle and I could tell from the look in his eyes that it would be the last time we would ever see one another. But because I was so young I eventually got over the fact of not having a father figure in my life, again.

I was glad to be living in the same house as my favorite cousin on my mom's side of the family. His name is Pooh and he was Tee's youngest child. Pooh was very spoiled and got whatever in the world he wanted. Maybe the fact that his oldest brother Tony was in prison for rape caused his mother to lavish her love upon him more heavily.

Tony, his brother, received a 40-year sentence for a crime that he really didn't commit. Him and one of his friends had been sexually involved with a white woman and when her husband found out, she screamed rape. In the early 1980's mixed couples were still an anomaly in the south. Tony declined the 8-year plea agreement the State offered him but his co-defendant accepted it. Tony told his mother that he couldn't accept the plea because the sex was consensual. Tee was brokenhearted from losing Tony, which caused her to shelter and protect Pooh.

Times were hard for us in the beginning. Especially around Christmas time. WhileTee spoiled Pooh, my mother did the best she could to make my sister and I smile.

Pooh knew how to manipulate my young mind.

Although he never played with his own toys and video games, he knew that I loved them. So whenever I would do something to make him angry, like not allowing him to practice his wrestling moves on me, or, not going to get him some water when he asked me, he would take his toys and games away from me. He did this to all the kids around him even his best friend Coolie. But I never held a grudge against Pooh because no matter what I did "wrong," he would eventually allow me to play with his toys and games again. When Tee took us shopping Pooh would even allow me to choose the toys and games that his mom purchased. So basically, his stuff was like mine anyway.

All situations have their pros and cons. And living under the same roof, as my aunt Tee, was definitely the most conning situation I've ever been in. She was the epitome of evil! All she cared about was herself and her two children. Everyone else was just pawns in her chess game, especially my mother. At one point in time my mother thought her sister really cared about her. But boy was she wrong!

When my mom was young, she and her other siblings (Lavetta, Lady, and Michael) witnessed Lady's father kill their mother and then himself in a jealous rage. Tee, who had control of the children's finances at that time, received a large portion of money. She took Lady in as her own while Lavetta and Michael went off to live with their dad. My mother ended up in Rosedale.

Tee was always all about money and for a long time she had all the money she could actually count. I can honestly say this woman has had a million dollars at one point in time. She used to be one of the biggest pill suppliers in Memphis. She supplied Delatans, Percocets, Morphine, and Xanax. All day long white people would come to her house to buy pills or to pawn off their valuables. I even witnessed some people who were hurting so bad for the drugs begging and crying for a fix. Tee would talk to those people like trash and she always wanted her money, no exceptions. But, she would allow some of the junkies to stay in her house while they broke their pills down into liquid form and injected it into their veins through the use of syringes.

Tee was what you would call bipolar. One minute, she would be clicking and saying that she wanted everybody out of her house, including us.The next minute she would be saying that we could stay. I couldn't stand her, but I did respect the fact that she was about her money.

I used to wonder why my mom didn't get in on the action with my aunt. But, to be honest, I don't believe that my aunt wanted my mother to be on her level. She wanted to keep my mom beneath her like a worker instead of treating her like family. Mama had a lot of love and respect for Tee. She wanted her to be like a mother figure to her so badly; she forgot that her own children needed her to be strong for them.

After our loss of Joe Lee, Mama eventually started dating again. She met a man name Chan who ended up being the biggest mistake that she ever made. At first Chan would come around and behave like a true gentleman, spending lots of time with my mom. But his gentlemanly veneer would prove to be nothing more than a polished act.

Mom had always been the rock to my sister and I and I wasn't quite ready for her to have another man in her life. But Chan eventually won both my mother's heart and mine. I'm not going to say my sister didn't get along with Chan, but I can admit she never liked him as much as she was crazy about Joe Lee.

Mom and Chan eventually landed a job together at a restaurant called "Shoney's." Mom began making incremental progress although we were still staying at Tee's house. She purchased her first car from Tee. It was a Dodge Dot and this car was what I call a real hooptie. It was an older modeled car with a bad oil leak and it smoked real badly. But even with all the complications, mom was very proud of her new car.

My sister and I used to hop into the car in the mornings so mom could drop us off at school. Boy, were we embarrassed! I would try to duck down in my seat while at the same time not get noticed by my mom for fear of being slapped. She would pull up in front of the school and make us get out. One morning the school principal came out with the fire extinguisher thinking my mom's car had caught fire. I was so humiliated! I eventually started waking my sister up earlier than usual in the a.m. telling her we could walk the couple of miles to school instead of riding along in that smoky, smelly car.

My mother never stopped flaunting her car no matter how bad it performed. When we would take the car back home to visit Rosedale we would have to stop at service stations and put water in the radiator and oil in the engine. Subsequently, a 2-hour drive became a 3-½ hour drive.

Even though Chan was an "Shade Tree" Mechanic, he never found the solution to the car problem and the engine finally gave out. When I heard the news I was the happiest child alive. My mom's second car was more acceptable for me; it was a Subaru with a digital dashboard and leather interior. This was the kind of car I didn't mind showing up to school and showcasing!

As my mother and Chan's relationship grew tighter,

the talk about them moving in together began to circulate. I was all game for the sudden change. After a few years of being mentally abused by Tee's up and down attitude, I couldn't wait to move out.

It was when I was 13 years old, in the year of 1993, my mom and Chan finally got an apartment and moved in together. Mom got a pay raise at work and the apartment and all of the bills were in her name. Although I was excited we moved out, I still would spend some nights at Tee's house. It was so big that half the time she didn't know if I was there or not.

My mother eventually got a promotion and became the Kitchen Supervisor. Now, the more money my mother made back then, the more she allotted to my sister and I for our allowance. She kept our pockets fat and never hesitated to spoil us. I love to dress so I put all of my money towards fashion. I was the slickest dresser in my classroom. Everything I wore had to match, from my shoestrings to my belt. My coordination game was on point!

Chan eventually began to grow envious of my mom's position. Although he had been given the Head Cook's position, he really wanted the Kitchen Manager spot that had been awarded to my mom. But, for the most part, Chan concealed his resentment. One would think that he would've been content with the fact that mom's position was bringing extra income into the home. But nope, not Chan, he was selfish and we would soon find out to what extent.

When payday came around Chan would give my mom his whole check. But later on at night he would always come back and ask for parts of it back. And sometimes he would even take the whole check back. Mom was so kindhearted that she would just hand it right back over to him. Even though mom's income alone was enough to handle all of the bills, Chan, as a man and her partner, should have been responsible enough to help her.

Chan's financial situation eventually grew worse. One day he had come home after spending his entire check. He claimed that he had a bad gambling habit and really needed some help. He was a real slick talker from Memphis. Us coming from Mississippi weren't used to fast talking city slickers like Chan and we didn't believe his claims. So my mother figured out a system to work around Chan's bad habit. Whenever Chan would give her his check she would immediately find something to spend it on. She would even try to lead by example by taking Chan along to witness her paying bills and purchasing important household items.

Then, we started to notice other strange things happening in our home. Things like waking up in the morning and realizing our microwave was missing only to have it reappear later on that night or the next day. Or, like when mom purchased her third car, a Ford Cougar, Chan would be at home with my mom but the new car would be gone. He would always claim that it was having some type of repairs done to it. Which made no sense because he was a "Shade Tree" Mechanic himself. He could do just about anything to a car except change out the engine or transmission. He even made money on the side doing odd repairs.

One day when my mom, sister, and I were inside the Cougar at a gas station some young guy ran up to our car and said, "I got what you need." He showed my mom a bunch of small white rocks and said he only wanted to keep the car for a few hours, and that he promised to bring it back on time. Mom told him that she had no idea what he was talking about. He proceeded to tell us that he drives our car all the time and that he recognizes it by its five-star rims. Boy, was my mother fuming! When we got back home she made Chan pack his belongings and move in with his mother.

Chan was a grown ass "momma's boy." He had his mother under the impression that my sister and I had been stressing him out causing him to relapse. He played on his mother's love for him to get money from her to pay his drug debts. And his mother never liked mine because she truly believed that my mom was the cause of her son's drug abuse.

Chan actually wasn't a bad guy until he fell victim to drug abuse. The U.S. has the highest incidence of cocaine abuse. It has been said that at least 1 out of 4 Americans between the ages 26 thru 34 have used cocaine in their lifetime, and the drug enforcement personnel estimated that about 2,500 Americans every day try cocaine for the first time. Cocaine and opiates have been popular since the 1800's (Wikipedia.org/Cocaine). And now methamphetamines have become more prominent. It's a very harsh reality but drugs destroy good people.

It wasn't long before Chan charmed his way back into our home and into my mom's life. He must have used his close proximity to my mom at work to get in her head and convince her to take him back. But, I strongly believe, he secretly held a grudge against my mom for putting him out. He seemed to play it cool and never revealed his hand just like the deceiver he was.

One morning I was awakened to a conversation. I overheard mom and Chan discussing the details about how they "pulled it off," and how no body was hurt. They talked about putting "Kevin's faggot ass part to the side," and calling Cool to give him his "take" for a job well done. I later found out that "Shoney's Restaurant," where mom and Chan worked, had been robed and everyone inside had been stripped of their valuables and cash. No one was ever

12

apprehended for the robbery.

Even though what mom and Chan did was wrong, it helped us to upgrade our living conditions. A few months later, we moved into a 3-bedroom brick home. This time all of the bills were in Chan's name. There were very few items in the house that belonged solely to mom.

3

The Encounters

Now, although my sister and I were spoiled I had begun to crave my own money. I really wanted a job but mom wouldn't allow it. She would always tell me, "Naw Jerry! What is it that you want that I haven't bought?" My relationship with mom was so close that I could tell her anything. And I mean anything! I even showed up one day in front of her with my penis in my hand, telling her something was wrong with me. I had an unbelievable itch that wouldn't go away.

Mom asked me if I was being sexually active and if so, did I know what condoms were? No was my answer to both questions. And when my mom took a closer look she soon realized what the problem was. It was similar to the issue that I had when I was six years old and there was a red ant biting me in the genital area. But this time it was a different kind of bug: crabs! They were everywhere! We had to get some special shampoo to treat it and when we did it was like a thousand of those things fell off of me. Boy, was I ashamed! I felt like a nasty dog! Every time I see one of those poor animals scratching away like crazy, I can imagine the feeling. I had to get rid of every pair of underwear I owned. And I never found out how I ended up infected.

I eventually began telling my mom that I was really taking a liking to girls, and that I wanted to have a girlfriend like my cousin Pooh. When I would spend nights at Pooh's house, there would be girls bringing him food and catering to his every need. The girls would also stay the night and

Pooh would make me sleep in the next room over. So, I would either pretend to sleep or stay up late playing "the game" and eaves dropping on Pooh's bedroom door. There would be moans coming from the girls.

So one day I asked Pooh what does he do with the girls in his bedroom. He said that I wasn't yet ready to learn. I told him that I was and explained my encounter with Gwen when I was 8 years old. Pooh didn't believe me at first but he eventually gave in to my questioning, and showed me some porn movies. He even told me how to please myself through masturbation. He said that the idea was to build up my stamina because girls didn't like dudes who ejaculated prematurely.

So once I mastered my craft, I started looking for my second prey. It came in the form of April Malone. My second sexual encounter was with her in 1994 and we would have our way with one another every little chance we got. She actually became a big part of my life late on into adulthood.

After that girls just started coming by the flock. Believe it or not I actually lost count! Boy, was I trifling! I got all kinds of girls pregnant. But I was still young. I was a child myself and I didn't want to slow down and raise a child. So I would have the girls abort the babies. And that is still one of my biggest regrets to this day, neglecting my responsibilities. I truly believe that karma haunts me all of the time even though I've asked God to forgive me.

After awhile April ended up breaking up with me. She got pregnant by a much older guy and they eventually got married. And although it bothered me for a while, it didn't stop me from having my way with other young girls my age at Trezevant High School, where I attended.

Tee's house was right across the street from Trezevant

15

High. Whenever I wanted to ditch school I would just leave the back door unlocked. My aunt Tee worked the graveyard shift at the largest hospital in Memphis called "The Med." When she got off work, she would send us off to school and then fall asleep and be out cold. Once she made sure we were off to school, she wouldn't come back downstairs, at least for some hours. So that gave us kids some time to sneak into the house and rendezvous during school hours.

Now, while mom and Chan were working out their differences, in our new home. I just couldn't stay away from Pooh. He always had something going on. Plus, he ended up getting a job at "Shoney's," where mom and Chan worked. And even though he had been spoiled all of his life, I actually witnessed him save up roughly $50,000 in his own paychecks. But Pooh didn't really need the money.

During the winter of 1994, we had a very bad ice storm. It was one of the biggest storms that would ever hit the city of Memphis. I remember it distinctly because of a very scary incident that occurred. The power was out for a week and one day my cousin Pooh, Chris, and I were walking from my house to Tee's house so I could spend the night. I was oblivious to the fact there had been two guys trailing behind us. Being as young as I was, I never expected what happened next. The guys got ground on us and stuck a pistol to Pooh's temple while the other guy waved his gun at Chris. They demanded our starter jackets. I was so afraid that I just froze. The guy with the gun on Pooh smacked him with the butt of his gun, which made me move a little faster. We quickly gave them our jackets and also our gym shoes. Later we learned that those same guys had been going around and robbing other people for their starter jackets, Michael Jordan gym shoes, and her herringbone necklaces.

The police were called and they took a police report.

16

But there was very little that we could tell them because the suspects had their faces covered. And would you believe our mothers went out and bought us brand new starter jackets! I ain't gone lie, I was too scared to wear mine.

The ice storm blew over and Spring fell towards the end of the school year. One day a group of us boys got together and agreed to go play some street basketball at one of our schoolmate's house named Cowboy. While we all headed towards his house I suddenly felt a punch to the side of my temple come from out of nowhere. It dazed me and caused me to stumble a little. When I looked up at my attacker, he stood way taller than me. I wondered what I had done to make someone that big punch me like that. I didn't know whether to run or try to defend myself and get punished even more. I was walking with like 12 other classmates and no one bothered to help me. I guess they thought they'd get beat too. Eventually my attacker ran off. When I told Pooh and Chris what happened they searched high and low for the culprit.

After that incident my mother enrolled me into a Tae Kwon Do class. It was the summer of 1995 and at first I was reluctant to take up martial arts because I thought it was only for the movies. But I enlisted anyway and so did my cousin Pooh. Mom said not only would I learn how to defend myself but it would also help me to control my attitude problem.

In the beginning of my martial arts classes I didn't like my instructor Ron Bosewell. He was a short white guy with glasses and I remember thinking, "Who he think he is, Chuck Norris?" During class I would display my dislike for him but he paid me no mind. It only caused him to make me workout extra hard. I thought that he was picking at me but it really helped me in the long run. Although the Tae Kwon Do classes took away from my other daily activities (basketball, video games, girls, etc.) it taught me how to defend myself.

4

Lessons Learned?

One day while I was sitting in the school cafeteria and conversing with some classmates, in walked the sexist girl that I had ever seen. We'll call her Marie; I knew that I had to have her at all cost. Not only was she beautiful but she also stayed fly. And so did I. I had also gained confidence in myself and believed that I could get this girl. And I wouldn't hesitate to use my Tae Kwon Do training in order to keep her.

Marie and I became an item and she had my nose wide open. She spoiled me to the fullest! Marie really believed in working and she would give me at least half of her work check, if not all of it, and allow me to spend it on whatever I wanted.

My sister ended up getting real close to Marie. This was odd because my sister wasn't good at maintaining relationships with other females. She wasn't a weirdo or anything she was just a loner. But her and Marie hit it off pretty well.

As soon as I felt like I had Marie wrapped around my finger, I began pursuing other females who were dumb enough to go to work and give me all of their money. My endeavors were successful for a while. I had a total of 8 females, with jobs, who felt good about giving me their money.

After consistently nagging my mom she eventually gave me a job at Shoney's as a part-time cook. My money together with the monies I would collect from females put me in position to buy myself everything I wanted. I wasn't as good as my cousin Pooh at stacking money. He believed in saving while I believed in spending. And that's exactly what I did.

I began to ask mom to buy me a car. I didn't have a driver's license, permit, nor did I know how to drive, but I was determined to learn. At first she told me no. Then she'd begin to say she would think about. And that was a good enough answer for me. I used to watch my cousin Pooh as he operated his first vehicle and navigated through traffic. He made it look so easy to where I thought it was a piece of cake. All I had to do was find someone dumb enough to let me take their car for a spin.

I eventually found a victim. Pooh's girlfriend, Tameka, stepped out on faith and allowed me to drive her grandmother's mini-van. Believe it or not, I didn't wreck it and I made very few mistakes. My only flaw was trying to back the car up. I eventually learned but it took me years. Whenever Tameka came over to Pooh's house I would convince him to have her let me drive whatever car she was in. I couldn't wait until she came over to cuddle with Pooh. I would drive off in her vehicle and be out late into the night. I never got in an accident but I did get pulled over once. I was in a zero tolerance area and the police said I looked suspicious. But they let me go with a warning.

Soon afterward, mom finally gave in and bought me a blue Mazda 626. I never got the opportunity to fully ride the car. It was beautifully, magnificent on the outside. It had deep-dish rims, an electronic sunroof, and a digital dashboard. But it was only a shell of a car that turned out to be a straight lemon. The seller had duped my mom and Chan, who was supposed to be a mechanic. Liquid glass had been put inside the engine, which seals the engine from gasket leaks and prevents it from smoking temporarily until the car is sold. These kinds of used auto sales never come along with warranties, so we basically took a loss.

I was back at square one stealing Tameka's car periodically. I eventually started stealing my mother's car at night while she was asleep. She was a very hard sleeper. I just had to make sure that I parked the car back in the exact same spot and position that she left it in before she went to bed.

But my car stealing days eventually came to an end. One night I stole mom's Cougar to impress this girl that I had a crush on named Danita Allen. We were out joyriding, speeding through a neighborhood called Skylake. I was on the way to my cousin Kee Kee's house to shoot the breeze with her. As I was approaching the house a female made a quick left turn in front of me and I smacked the back of her car.

I panicked, jumped out of the car screaming at the girl saying, "Look what the hell you did to my car!"

She was hysterical and kept saying, "I'm sorry! I'm sorry!" over and over again. She said that since she was at fault and she would pay for it. I was thinking "Damn right you gone pay for it." But how could I explain this to my mother?"

The police were called and since I was an underage driver with no real I.D. I had no other choice but to face the moment of truth and call mom. I told her what happened and she had very little time to get there before the police. I asked her to have Pooh come and switch places with me. He had a legit driver's license plus everyone thought that he and

I looked alike.

Mom discussed the idea with Tee and she agreed. So mom, Pooh, and Tee made it to the accident scene before the Cops. Pooh and I switched clothes and hoped the driver of the other vehicle wouldn't notice. She was so bus crying and trying to explain what happened to her parents, she never even paid attention. Either that or the saying must be true: "all blacks look alike." But it didn't matter to me as long as I escaped the bullet. Pooh saved my ass that day.

For a while my mom wouldn't say very much to me. But once her insurance company gave her enough money to put down on another car her attitude towards me lightened up. She went and bought a Candy Apple Red Delta '88. It was beautiful and I enjoyed being seen in it. And believe it or not, my mother actually began to let me drive it! Like I've said, I have a very good mother.

Mom started allowing me to have female company at the house. She told me she would rather me entertain them in the house, under her discretion, than to sneak out and have something bad happen. But even though my mom was cool with it, Chan was not. He would try to flirt with the girls I brought around! Sometimes he would even tell them that I was a player and that I always had different girls in and out of the house.

Chan's attitude towards my sister and I grew worse. I don't know if it was because of his drug abuse or not, but he couldn't stand us. In my opinion, it was for no reason at all. One day mom let me keep the car to drive my sister and I to school. So I wanted to impress this girl that I was fooling around with, name LaKendria Williams. She lived on our same street and her and I would later have a son together. She went to the same school as my sister and I so I told her to come over and she could ride to school with us.

I guess Chan got angry that mom allowed me to keep the car when he needed it to go to work that morning. So he called his mom for a ride. 30 minutes after I was dressed and ready to go I began to wonder what was taking LaKendria so long. I went to the front door to see if she was walking towards the house. Chan's mom was sitting in her car in front of the house and when I looked towards the driveway I saw someone under my mother's car. I must have startled him when I opened the door because Chan came from under mom's car with some red fluid on his hand. He got into his mother's car and they drive off.

I didn't think much about seeing him under the car until we were driving down Northmeade, the street that we lived on. There was a hill at the end of Northmeade that led to a four lane cross street called Rangeline. I tried to slow down but the car wouldn't stop. I had my foot smashed all the way down on the brakes and nothing happened. We were headed right out into the middle of school traffic! I refused to be the reason that we all lost our lives that day. So I did the only thing that I could possibly think of. I threw the car into park and jumped the curb into somebody's front yard. It worked! I got the car stopped and got us out of that situation unharmed. The front passenger side tire took some damage but everything else was fine.

After we got the car back to the house we noticed that there was a puddle of red liquid in the driveway where Chan had cut the brake line. I told my mother that I had seen Chan under her car earlier that day but she still stayed with him. I don't know what he could have told my mom to make her stay with him after he tried to kill her only two children. I lost all respect for him after that and I really wanted some way to get revenge. I knew that I couldn't take him physically because even though he smoked crack he was a very strong dude who maintained his physical stature.

My mom, sister and I were still living under Chan's roof. Everything was in his name and he continuously reminded us of that. And eventually the things that disappeared from the house would never return. First it was the microwave, then the T.V., and then even the living room furniture set. And this was a very nice brand new living room set with a leather reclining couch, a three piece table set, and I mean I could go on and on about this piece of furniture. One day after school it was just gone. Chan's drug addiction just kept getting worse. He even resented my mom who was the very person who stuck by his side through it all. I tried to rationalize it in my young mind by asking myself "what kind of drug could make a person not want to have anything; no money, no car, no furniture, or even a good woman?"

While mom was going through her personal relationship problems, I finally got the chance to experience my own in 1996. My girlfriend Marie who I was so crazy about broke my heart. Now, I was never a saint with her but her being my #1 girl, I never thought she would dish me out a taste of my own medicine.

One day I spent the night over my cousin Pooh's house and the phone rang. It was my cousin Chris' girlfriend, Shagema. I picked up the phone and the conversation went as follows:
Me: "Hello."
Shagema: "Can I speak to Chris?"
Me: "He ain't here Shagema."
Shagema: "Oh, ok. Have you talked to Marie?"
Me: "Naw." Why you asking bout her?" "She don't fuck wit you."
Shagema: "What you mean she don't fuck with me?

Well did the bitch tell you she fucked Too Too?"

Me: Yeah right, quit playing."

Shagema: "I ain't lying, and you can tell her I said it, too!"

Now, I was only kidding with Shagema but evidently she was serious.

Too Too was someone whom I had began calling my friend. In fact, Too Too, Emerie, Mark, and I would hang out all of the time after school. So when Shagema hit me with the news I was crushed. I called Too Too and let him know how I felt about the situation but I soon learned in life that "men will be men." Too Too and I actually remained friends. But I wasn't friendly with Marie after that. I ended up being physically abusive towards her. I know that real men don't hit women but believe me it took a long time for me to learn this lesson in life. Actually, Marie wouldn't be the only woman that I'd put my hands on.

It seemed as if Marie had a way of bringing out the worst in me. But I was head over heels for her and we kept on dating. I had lost all respect for her so I courted a lot of other girls at the same time. I'm aware that two wrongs don't make a right but I was young and that's how I dealt with things at that time. The pain caused me to be hard on females. Plus, Too Too and I discontinued our relationship. There was no love lost but if the shoe was on the other foot, I wouldn't have done it to him.

5

When It Rains, It Pours

My senior year in high school was supposed to be my breakout year and I was preparing to graduate. Marie and I were on all right terms but she was completely irate because I had gotten LaKendria pregnant. LaKendria had already had two abortions because of me but she wasn't letting anyone talk her out of this pregnancy. I just had to figure out some way to suck up to Marie while preparing to be a father at the same time.

Once again, I turned to my mother for her wisdom. I asked her how could I keep my relationship with Marie strong while bringing a child into the world by another young lady. Mom divulged a shocking revelation. She said that she found out that Chan had fooled around with another woman at their job. I was completely unaware but mom had noticed the signs. And to make matters worse she was a white woman! This turned my mother's world upside down. To be honest, I don't think that she ever recovered from the disappointment.

My mother didn't raise us to be racist, but my mother was very close to my cousin Tony before he was wrongfully accused and sentenced to prison. He was convicted for a crime that he never committed, the rape of a white woman. Not only did mom lose her cousin but also her friend. So in mom's eyes Chan had committed the ultimate act of betrayal by sleeping with a white woman. And to make matters worse it was a woman that she worked with, She was upset, depressed, and not to mention, embarrassed in front of all her coworkers.

Mom thought that if she confronted Chan with his infidelity it would cause him to leave the woman alone. But not only did he continue the relationship, he also kicked us out of his home! I remember that day vividly. It was pouring down raining outside and I could hear mom cursing at Chan. And all I heard next was Chan screaming "Pack ya'll shit and get out of my house! As a matter of fact, I'm packing ya'll shit for ya'll!"

After he put us out into the rain with all of our belongings and nowhere to go, we ended up back in the same place where we started from, Tee's house. Tee had mom thinking that she had her back and vowed to help her get back on her feet. But that never happened. Honestly, things just got worse. Mom's work performance began to decline. She was dedicated to her job and her position as the Kitchen Manager but she was zoning out at work. For her to see Chan flaunting around the work place with his new woman was crushing her spirit.

Tee knew that my mom was hurting. She was a big pill dealer so she always had junkies and crack heads lingering around her house. There was one in particular named Sherie. This woman had beautiful features and maintained her nice toned body. Mom would come in contact with Sherie often. And boy did Sherie love to smoke crack! One day I came home from school and saw mom sitting at the top of the stairs looking zoned out. I knew that something was wrong because she wouldn't look me in my eyes. Plus, her hair was wild all over her head and she loved her hair. She used to keep it in a shoulder length Jheri-curl style, so to see it all dried up was out of the ordinary.

The next thing that came out of my mouth was a slip

up. I asked her if she was on drugs. I wasn't expecting the answer that I received. Mom shook her head up and down. It crushed the shit out of me! There I was in the 12th grade with a baby on the way, my sister had just had her first child, Demain, we were living in the very place we had all dreaded coming back to, AND my heart and soul had just told me she was a drug user. Damn! When it rained, it poured!

I was lost and confused. I remembered how we used to make fun of Chan for selling our household appliances for drugs and claiming he had a gambling problem. I couldn't understand, for the life of me, why my mother would want to take herself down that same road. All that was running through my head was how the strongest woman I know was now a crack head? Right there on those stairs that day my life was changed forever.

I later found out that Sherie was the person who introduced mom to crack. She told her, the crack would make all of her pains go away. What she didn't tell her was, she would be chasing that same high 20 years later. What really surprised me was Tee was mom's supplier. When mom stopped coming home from work at night I would go out looking for her. When I couldn't find her I'd go ad ask Tee if she knew mom's whereabouts. She'd act as if she was concerned, too, but she really knew where my mother was the whole time.

My sister and I were negatively affected by mom's drug abuse. We ended up dropping out of school. Not physically, but mentally. We'd show up to school but our minds' just weren't into anymore.

I confided in my girlfriend Marie and she did the best she could to console me. She even gave me $1,000.00 to put down on my own car before she even had her own. But driving wasn't even fun for me anymore. My mother's drug abuse was a dagger in my heart and all I wanted to do was die. I just didn't have the guts to kill myself.

Pooh eventually found his way and went off to college while me and my family lived with his mom and listened to her talk negatively about us to anyone who would listen. I mean, you wouldn't even think that she was our family by listening to her. Pooh absolutely resented my mom for some reason.

One day, out of the blue, Tee had her husband Brandon do her dirty work for her. He told us that we had a week to move out, what a low blow! Talk about kicking people while they were down! Where were we supposed to get the money for a down payment on a new place to live? My mother wasn't even in her right frame of mind!

We packed up our few belongings and moved into an Extended Stay Suite that had a bi-weekly rate of $345.00. Mom didn't last long at "Shoney's" so her and I got new jobs at the Eagle Nest Sports Bar and Grill. The new job paid us weekly.

Our one bedroom hotel room was extremely crowded. My sister was raising Demain and she was pregnant with her second child. So between my sister, her son, my mom and me, guess who had to sleep on the floor.

Mom's check was barely enough to cover the weekly rate but it helped for about two months. Then one day when it was time to pay the rent she just disappeared. Consequently, my sister, my nephew, and I were stuck with nowhere to go. I packed up our few belongings and we laid our heads wherever someone would allow us.

When we finally caught up with mom she had spent half of her check, probably on drugs. And I couldn't believe who she was with, Chan! Now Chan had a smoking partner in my mom. I would sometimes find them at crack houses in woods that had no utilities. They both would be looking a mess.

Mom informed my sister and I she wanted to leave Memphis and head back to Mississippi. But to be honest that was something that I didn't want to do. It was completely out of the question for me. But eventually mom and my sister decided to go and live with mom's sister in St. Paul, Minnesota. I was all game for that move. I thought that my aunt in St. Paul would embrace us, help my mom to kick her habit, and restore our family back to normal. But boy was I mistaken!

Mom broke a way from Chan for good this time. And her and my sister agreed to catch a bus up to St. Paul and start over. I would stay behind and try to find my own way by mainly staying at one of my female friend's, named Karla, house.

The trip wound up a disaster. Once they arrived in St. Paul, my sister immediately reported the bad news to me. My aunt who lived in St. Paul was also using crack and her house was a known crack hangout. I won't go into further detail but trust me it was bad.

Meanwhile I had worked out something with Tee and moved back in. In spite of all that she put us through, I still went back and agreed to pay her $100.00 a week. I needed a stable place to live while I prepared for my son to be born.

I began to hangout around the neighborhoods a lot and got exposed to gang activity. One of my close associates caught a murder charge on one of our homies. I never fully knew the details but it was such a devastating tragedy. Two lives wasted, one to the prison system and the other to the grave.

Young men mostly fall victim to gangs when their fathers are absent from their lives. Young males need other male figures in their lives to help mold their character and teach them how to be men. And when there is no father figure in the home, young men look to the streets and their fellow peers for guidance. The gang then takes the place of the dominant male figure and provides stability, guidance, and acceptance. But gangs never really have the best interest of the youth at heart. Usually the youth only end up more misguided.

I was no exception.

6

The "Solution"

I eventually found a niche. It was negative and extreme, but it was normal in the kind of community that I grew up in. All I needed was a gun and a ski mask.

I held on to the memory of mom and Chan discussing a heist in our living room. They talked about how no one was hurt and about the amount of money they received. I was starting to see the apple doesn't fall far from the tree, because my mind was set on the same thing.

I told myself that my next move would be my best move. I began casing out the place where I worked. I took notes on how to open the safe and when to expect large amounts of money to be present, And once I had it planned all out, all I needed next was the right players for the job.

I found three dudes who I knew would keep their mouths closed. And let's just say that the robbery was successful. The money was great and no one got hurt. But it was like the "Robbery Fever" struck me; all I wanted to do was rob. I felt like a kind of Robin Hood figure, robbing from the rich and giving to the poor. I wouldn't rob individuals on the street for their jackets and shows like someone had done to me some years prior. I wanted the safe! I wanted it all!

Our next lick proved to be successful, also. We had a homeboy that worked in the Raleigh Springs Shopping Mall named Lil' D. I approached Lil' D wit' the opportunity

31

of a lifetime; well, at least that's what I told him any way. I asked him if he wanted to make some extra cash before the Christmas holidays rolled around, "Hell Yeah!" Lil' D replied. I told him all he had to do was leave the side door open to his job the next time he took the trash out. Then one of my other comrades and me would come in and stick the place up. We would use a little extra aggression towards Lil' D to make sure no one suspected him of being involved.

The place was called K&B toy store. It was extremely crowded because it was the holiday season, December of 1998. The mall was packed with customers so that store was loaded with cash! Everything went according to our plan. I informed Lil" D that the investigators would try to find out if it was an inside job but if he just stuck to his role as a victim everything would be okay. Boy was I wrong!

Three days after the robbery, some detectives knocked on Tee's door and asked for me by my name. They took two of my other accomplices and me into custody. And guess whom we saw already in intake? Lil' D! After all of the prep talking that I did he still gave us all up. He claimed that the cops scared him into snitching.

I was charged with Aggravated Robbery and my bond was set $20,000.00. I was scared as hell! I didn't know anything about how the whole process would go but I did know that I couldn't come up with 20 grand to get out of jail. I was stuck!

I made my free phone call and called Marie. I told her I was in custody at the county jail and I wanted to get out badly. Marie called a few bail bonding companies and found one that would take $1,020 and her co-signature to get me out. She explained to me how the bonding process worked. The bail bonding companies will get people out of jail for 10% of the amount of the actual bond. They would take 5% if you had the money available immediately.

Since Marie was only a waitress at the time making two dollars and 15 cents plus tips, we didn't have the money. But she knew that I wanted to get out fast so she acted fast. She worked 7 days a week plus stole tips from other waitresses. She was able to bond me out before these Christmas holidays.

I got out of jail broke with no job. But I needed some money to hire a lawyer because Aggravated Robbery was automatic jail time. So I went back to hustling females out of their paychecks in order to come up with attorney fees.

My mom ended up moving back to Memphis after my arrest. No matter what kind of problems she would be faced with, she would always have my back. She would always do the best that she could to help me in whatever way she could.

One would think that after catching a serious charge I would have learned my lesson. Well, I didn't. It only enticed me to want to rob even more and in the summer of 1999, I got my chance.

A partner of mine had been telling me about the Ace Check Cashing place on Watkins Street. He said on Fridays the place was always jammed packed with people cashing their paychecks. Plus, the girls that worked there looked like easy marks that would more than likely give the cash up quickly with no protests. So, I immediately began formulating a plan. I sent Karla into "Ace" a couple of times in order to get a lay out of the place. She mentioned she had gotten the same feeling about the employees that my partner had gotten and she felt like it would be a sweet lick.

I wanted to do the robbery close to the first of the month. I explained our get away route to all of the participants and picked a particular Friday to make our move. On the day of the robbery, Kayla went in to case the place once more while making an actual business transaction so she wouldn't look suspicious. Also, when the detectives rolled back the cameras she wouldn't stand out. And when the coast was clear my partner and I entered the business with hoodies over our heads, bandanas over the bottom portion of our face, and our guns drawn.

We caught the teller completely off-guard, kicked back in her chair, and yapping away on the phone. Once she realized what was happening she screamed, dropped the phone and pressed a panic button. I wasn't expecting for that to happen so I did the first thing that came to mind; I tried to haul ass right out of the back door and my partner was right behind me. But, the door wouldn't open!

The panic button had sounded on alarm and simultaneously locked us inside of the lobby. My partner stuck his pistol up to the Plexiglas and told the teller that if she didn't open the door than he would start shooting. So she pressed the button again and opened the door, saving us from going back to jail on another robbery charge.

After our failed attempt we fell back for a while. But I had lawyer fees to pay plus a son to raise. I had to think of something quick. All I needed was one more good robbery and I could be done with all of this crap before somebody got seriously hurt. But the score had to be big.

What could I rob that would set me straight for a while? Some thing that would enable me to pay my lawyer, get my own place to stay, and sustain me until I found another job? The only thing that kept coming to my mind was a bank, and there was a bank almost on every corner, so it wouldn't be hard to pick one. I just had to make sure that it was one with no Plexiglas and had a smooth getaway route.

I ended up finding the perfect one. It was the Union Planters back on Frayser Boulevard. This bank was literally 10 minutes walking distance from Tee's house! All I needed was some manpower and the perfect getaway driver because this had to be done to perfection.

For the next two months I did an extensive reconnaissance on the bank. On the outside of the bank there was a lady security guard who did her rounds every two hours. I sent Karla to case the inside to tell me how many tellers there were. She reported that there were four at the front counter and one that worked the drive through window.

The bank had a front and a side entrance. There was a tire company next door. I decided that we would use the side entrance because it would allow us to blend in with the traffic that was coming and going from the tire company.

Once I learned the Bank Manager always arrived an hour earlier than the other employees then that was the last piece of information that I needed. The only thing I was worried about was the lady security guard. She had a big ass gun on her hip! And I'm pretty sure she had received the proper training on how to shoot it.

Like I stated earlier, I needed someone who was just as crazy as I was to help me pull off this suicide mission. So I approached a few dudes whom I knew were bad asses. But, when I mentioned bank robbery they clammed up. But I didn't let that hold me back. Eventually an old partner of mine whom I had done some previous robberies with was game. Plus, I know that Karla would come through because of the love that she had for me. I also used my younger cousin Lil' Willie as my third gunman.

Next I had to find some wheels. An associate of mine sold me a stolen Ford Taurus that we would use as the getaway car. Karla was our getaway driver. I had her park the getaway car near a wooded area behind the store Festival Wigs on Rangeline Street, I instructed her to drop us off and to wait exactly four minutes at the rendezvous point for us to come running through the woods. If she didn't see us in four minutes she was to drive off, ditch the car and go to her aunt's house in Ridge Crest where she could watch the news to see if we were caught and wait on my phone call.

I wanted the timing of the robbery to be perfect, so we waited until December of 1999. It was exactly one year from the K&B toy store robbery I just knew that bad luck wouldn't strike me twice.

On the second Friday of the month my two accomplices and I entered the Union Planters Bank on Frayer Boulevard. With our guns drawn we demanded that the tellers started filling up bags with money. I told them I didn't want any funny business like dye packs or panic buttons.

The female security guard was doing her round on the opposite side of the building from where we would exit. So I figured that by the time she made it back around to our side we would already be gone. So after receiving the cooperation of the employees we made our exit at full speed. The next thing I know, Pow! Pow! Pow! I looked over my shoulder and saw the lady security guard firing her gun at us and playing hero to someone else's money.

I saw my cousin go down and I thought he was hit. My partner covered us and started firing back. After checking to make sure that my cousin was okay, we made our way through the wooded area. Karla was there, waiting patiently. Once we entered the car she kissed me and said "You know I wasn't gone leave you."

After ditching the car and getting rid of our clothes we went to Tee's house to split up the proceeds. I knew she wasn't home because she had picked up a serious gambling habit and had been going to the casino spending nights gambling. So I thought that we had the house to ourselves but like I said before Tee always had some type of junkie 'round. And while we were discussing the bank robbery a junkie named Ben who had been living at Tee's house eavesdropped on our conversation. Ben then went and reported the information to Tee.

A few days went by and the news had been buzzing hard about the robbery. They reported that the suspects had disappeared into thin air. So far the investigators had no leads. Up until the robbery I had never had more than $1,500 at one time. But my take from the holdup was roughly $6,000! I went out and paid down on a 1993 ES 300 Lexus. It was black and grey with black leather interior. I purchased some rims and a few T.V.'s to be installed. I felt like I was really doing it big at a time. I thought I had it all.

About a week went past without incident. Then one night Karla and I was lying together when the breaking news hit. There was an F.B.I. agent on the T.V. talking about how they were closing in on the suspects and would have the investigation complete within a couple of days.

I didn't realize that we had hit a Federal Bank. But it didn't really matter because it sounded as if the Feds were about to take down someone else for our crime. But actually, the Federal Agent was talking about us! The agent was telling us that our days were numbered. But I was so naïve to the fact, I just kept on balling and spending money.

One day I was getting my sound system and T.V.'s installed in my car by a guy, who I'll call Whiteboy, in Tee's driveway. I had made a run across the street to the Rangeline apartments and on my way back I saw maybe 20 or more F.B.I. and A.T.F. agents in Tee's yard surrounding Whiteboy. I was scared shitless!

I started walking down the street in the opposite direction while trying to figure out a way out of the hood. I made it to a phone and called my cousin Marlo. He picked me up and I gave him the rundown on what I had done. When I explained to him what kind of heat I was under I could tell that he didn't want any parts of it. So, I had him to drop me off at my cousin Kee Kee's house. Now Kee Kee knew all about what I had done. He was one of the first people that I had asked to rob the bank with me. Although his answer was "No," I knew that he wouldn't tell anyone or turn me in.

Marlo dropped Kee Kee and I off at Kee Kee's friend's house. I didn't know about the F.B.I.'s ability to utilize technology to apprehend potential suspects. So as soon as I got into the house I used the phone to call my sister. She told me not to come back because it was hot. The Feds had placed a transmitter on Tee's phone and less than 10 minutes after making the call, they had me in custody.

I ended up back in jail on another Robbery charge. The Detectives told me that I had really screwed up this time and made it into the big league. But at the time I didn't understand what they meant. I was booked and processed and my bond was set at $50,000. I figured that it couldn't have been that bad with a bond so low. Once I hit the second floor of the Memphis County Jail, located at 201 Poplar, the guys already knew who I was from watching the news. I didn't know if I should've tried to post bail or just wait to see if the Feds would try to pick up the case.

After sitting in jail for a month, I had Marie post my bail on January 14, 2000. She had gotten an apartment in Hillsdale with her roommate. I lived there with them for the seven days that I was out. My plan was to hire the same lawyer who was working on my first case and see what kind of deal he could get me for both cases.

On January 21, 2000, Marie left for work in the morning. It was my birthday so I had planned to swing through and holler at my moms and sister. Moms said she was going to bake my favorite cake: triple layered lemon with lemon frosting, Mom was a cake specialist and I couldn't wait to sink my teeth into it. There was a knock at the door. Instead of looking through the peephole to see who it was, I just opened it up. And there they were, F.B.I. Agents. "Kendrick, there you are!" said one of the Agents. "We didn't give you a bond to make, but we're about to take you to a place where you'll never get a bond: the Clifford Davis building on front street."

When I arrived at the building and was taken in front of the Magistrate, I could smell power. The United States of America had indicted me on Bank Robbery and I could sense, I wouldn't be released until I served my time first, Boy was I sick!

My bond was denied and I was considered a flight risk. Then I was whisked off to the C.C.A. Federal holding facility in Mason, Tennessee. I was booked, processed, and given my Federal number 17156-076. The place felt like a prison with all of the barbed wire fences that surrounded it. They took me to my permanent housing area called I-Dorm, where there was like 65 beds lined up side by side.

The showers were out in the open and there were like

8 stalls separated by small cubical walls where we had to take shits. The sinks were directly in front of each toilet so a person could easily walk by and see you using the restroom. I was being exposed to a whole other league and in due time I would actually see how cut throat the Federal System was. It was all very uncomfortable and took some time to get accustomed to.

7

The Reality

I didn't know anybody so for the first few weeks I stayed to myself and just observed everything around me. There were all kinds of rumors floating around about inmates jumping on other people's cases or testifying on their friends in order to get time cuts. The judge had even told me at my second court appearance not to discuss my case because guys could testify and use that information against me. And if the information was valuable, the persons could receive some relief off of their sentence if the government put in the recommendation for 5K-1. I was speechless! I wasn't used to hearing shit like that, it was all new to me.

I didn't know anything about sentencing guidelines at that time I found out the Judge didn't really have any power and the Prosecutor would file a "Motion" or made some sort of "Request," then 9 ½ times out of 10, the Judge would honor and go along with it.

I knew the situation was more serious than I thought when my State Attorney told me that I'd be better off just getting a Public Defender because all he'd do as a State Attorney is over charge me and the results would be the same. So I ended up using a Court Appointed Lawyer named Ralph L. Johnson.

Mr. Johnson was very honest with me and told me that Bank Robberies could range from White Collar crimes all the way up to Violent Offenses. He informed me that my case didn't qualify as a White Collar offense because weapons were used and discharged during the robbery. He felt that my only hope was I'd get a decent Pre-Sentence Investigator (P.S.I.), who wouldn't find all sorts of technical reasons to make my sentencing range extremely long.

Mr. Johnson told me that my other option was to inform the Government about some other crimes that haven't been solved yet. And if the information was substantial enough I could be recommended for what they call a "Downward Departure."

Basically, they wanted me to snitch. I asked Mr. Johnson if I snitched about unsolved crimes did he have any idea how that would make me look throughout the jail system? And who would protect my family? He flat out told me that no one would protect my family and that would be a risk I would just have to take. He said they might even use my information, not feel it is valid enough, and still not cut me a deal.

Now, all of this was really irrelevant information to me because I would have never considered snitching in the first place. Snitches are weak individuals who should have never been involved in the game in the first place. We should never indulge in something that we wont be able to deal with the consequences that may come later. So that was the end of that discussion.

We moved on to the next option. The Government would allow me the opportunity to receive a three-point deduction from my sentencing guidelines for accepting responsibility for my crime and not forcing them to go to trial. It was common knowledge that the conviction rate in the Feds is like 97%. Only 1 out of 1,000 cases are won in trial against the Feds. So I told Mr. Johnson to let me get through the P.S.I. stage first and I would think about it.

While in the Federal facility I ended up connecting with a few dudes out of Nashville: Big Zell, Ed, and Calloway. They were all in on drug related charges but Calloway was involved in a big cocaine conspiracy. The guy that the Feds really wanted was name P-Dub. P-Dub was kept in a separate facility from the rest of all of his co-defendants because a lot of them were willing to snitch on him for lighter sentences. But not Calloway! He talked about P-Dub all of the time. I mean he talked about him so much that at one point in time I questioned his sexuality. But later on I found out that he just really looked up to P-Dub's movements and how he ran his drug operation in Nashville.

Ed and Zell showed me the ropes about keeping my business to myself. They told me that if anyone asked me what I was in for, just make up a lie. And that's exactly what I did. One day two guys named Zig and Big Head had returned back from court. They claimed that my Co-defendant was at 201 Poplar saying that I had snitched on him. Obviously his accusations were false. We haven't even gotten our paperwork back yet!

My mom and sister were still living at Tee's house. And one day when I called home they told me some very disturbing news. Mom was doing laundry when she discovered a large sum of cash and some Crime Stoppers information about the Bank Robberies. Damn it! My aunt had turned me in! This woman must have had a demon in her or something. She was a major pill supplier but she turned in her own family member for a measly thousand dollars that she didn't even get to spend because my mom and sister kept the money.

I later found out that there were also three more people who called Crime Stoppers. I found out the names of the callers but I promised my sources that I wouldn't reveal their names. Crime Stoppers is an anonymous hotline where individuals can call in and report (snitch) crimes under the cloak of anonymity. I was done with Tee for good. To this day we still haven't spoken to one another. She ended up admitting in Church that she called and turned me in. She may have thought that she ruined me. But, little did she know, I would become one of the biggest marijuana suppliers in the city of Memphis.

I threw my X-Box in the water and soaked the game. Every time someone talked about drugs I had my ears wide open. I wanted to know about all of the pros and cons, and I knew that the right person would provide it. Calloway loved to talk. Even though he wasn't a key figure, he still gave me a lot of details. I soaked up all of the knowledge that he gave me. And since I was the youngest person in the dorm at that time he gave me the nickname Juvenile, or Juvie. Some people still call me that to this day.

Shortly after I did my P.S.I., I was sentenced and a week later I began my prison stint. Zig and I both got there on the same day. He was a cool guy but much older than me. So when we hit the Compound we both went our separate ways.

The Compound didn't look like what I thought a prison would look like. It looked more like a college campus. All the inmates had their clothes ironed and starched, and wore shiny boots. The dorms were spotless with T.V.'s everywhere. The Correctional Officers (C.O.) addressed you as Mister and used your last name. They would be like "Mr. Watson, you're wanted in the Counselor's Office," or "Mr. Watson, your work assignment is..." etc. They treated you with the upmost respect.

The Feds give out a lot of time and they don't have

a parole system. So it is basically home for half of the inmates there. So the system is setup for the inmates to live as comfortable as possible. They had a real store on the Compound for us to purchase our commissary from. The Dining Hall was setup like Ruby Tuesdays, complete with salad bars and desserts. And the food was A-1!

What blew me away was the Educational Department. At F.C.I. in Memphis if you had a High School diploma or G.E.D. you could apply for college. There was a program through Southwest Community College where you could actually receive an Associates Degree. Professors would come and teach classes at night.

There was also an alternative option for those who had their G.E.D. or High School Diploma, Unicor. Unicor is a factory inside of the Federal Prison System. They produce everything from cable wire and furniture to different kinds of Military equipment. Everybody wanted to work in Unicor, because it had a much higher pay rate than any other job on the Compound. I've actually seen guys making up to $700.00 a month working in Unicor. That kind of income enabled them to send money home for their children. But the waiting list for Unicor was extremely long. And my personal problem was I had dropped out of school, so my chances of getting into Unicor and making some decent money was out of the question. But I did add my name to the waiting list.

My next move was to get my G.E.D. It was a feat that I achieved within five months of being on the Compound. And while I waited for my name to be called for Unicor I got a job on the yard crew. It was a job that I never had to work because I paid other inmates to sign my name on the role-call as if I had shown up for work.

The currency in the Feds was mailing stamps. Each

stamp was worth a quarter and a whole book of them was worth $5.00. Stamps could get you anything that you needed; like certain foods, shoes shined, clothes ironed, or even someone smashed for violating. No matter who you were on the streets or how much money you had, you couldn't control the Compound if you didn't have all of the stamps.

Marie would come to visit me and I'd fill her in on the ways of prison life. I found out that the Correctional Officers in the visiting room were extremely relaxed. They let us sit next to our family and they had a playroom for the children. We could also purchase picture tickets and take as many pictures as we liked.

The prison phone system was setup to allow us to use 300 minutes a month. Each call lasted for a 15-minute duration. I loved talking on the phone. It was my biggest weakness and would eventually bring me down.

I would use my 300 minutes in the first 5-7 days of each month talking to Marie or my son's mother LaKendria. Talking to them helped my time go by smoothly and helped me to stay focused. I knew I had to keep them on my team. They both were relatively young and doing time wasn't something they were used to, especially knowing that I would be gone for more than two years.

In the beginning both LaKendria and Marie made sure my Commissary Account stayed straight. But I was spending big, instead of saving for a rainy day. I was spending the money just as fast as it was put on my books. One day while on a visit I told Marie that I wanted to start making my own money. She asked me how and I told her by selling marijuana. She asked how I would get it and I told her that she would have to bring it to me. All I had to do was find someone that I could trust to sell it for me, while I would supply the product, and we'd both make a profit.

Marie was reluctant with my idea at first. I was in a Federal Prison and if she got caught we'd both receive additional Federal charges. So I knew that I had to plan carefully. But once I got her gamed and ready to go, all I had to do was find a pusher. Meanwhile, I had started to hang out with a few Gangsta Disciples Members named Bear, Los G, and Smut. They were cool but I never really felt a trustworthy vibe from them.

I had to run the idea by my cellmate named Poole. I told him that I wouldn't run the cell hot and that if all went according to plan he would never have to buy Commissary again. I would pay for everything. He was more excited about the idea than I was. Poole even suggested a person who might want to sell the weed for me and keep me in the clear. He brought the guy to me and we shook hands and came to an agreement.

Now I was faced with three more problems. First, who would I get the weed from? Secondly, how would I get it in through the visiting room? And my third problem was, I didn't have a clue about quantities and prices.

A person, whom I'll call J-Dogg, told me marijuana was sold in prison by the Chapstick caps. A Chapstick cap is stuffed with weed and sold for $25.00 or five books of stamps. J-Dogg would keep $5.00 off of each sale and give me the other $20.00.

He also told me the best way to get the weed in. I would have to have the Mule fix the weed up by breaking it down real fine, taking out all of the sticks and seeds, and putting it into individual balloons. Then I would have to have my visitor buy some M&M's and put the weed balloons in the pack. Then they'd have to buy me a drink but in reality I'd be swallowing the balloons.

I found a guy that used to date my sister who sold me the weed. I never let him know that I didn't have a clue about prices. I wrote him a letter in code asking him what "three trunks" went for. We had to watch what we said in our outgoing letters in the Feds because we weren't allowed to seal it up. The C.O.'s had the option to read what we had written if they so desired. And a lot of the C.O.'s that worked on the graveyard shift would read the inmates mail just to pass time.

J-Dogg told me to ask the supplier about ounces and that's what I did. I didn't know if the prices he gave me were correct or not. I just wanted to sell something and live like a King in jail.

My first tryout was a disaster! I didn't get caught but I found out that swallowing balloons wasn't as simple as I thought. I was damn near swallowing 20 balloons and gagging and almost hurling. I thought I was going to pass out! I began to think it wasn't worth it. Plus, Marie was afraid and thinking that the C.O.'s would notice my actions.

But we actually made it through. And when I got back to the dormitory I asked J-Dogg how I was supposed to get the balloons out of me. He told me that I'd have to stick my finger down my throat until I threw them up. Now I was really questioning if it was worth it or not. I really didn't want to play in my own vomit but I guess this was the price you had to pay when you wanted to smuggle illegal contraband into a Federal Prison.

So I forced myself to throw-up until nothing else would come out of me. I only ended up with 18 balloons even though I had swallowed 26. But I couldn't really remember so I called my supplier and he confirmed that he had indeed sent 26. So I told J-Dogg that I still had some balloons stuck inside of me. He exclaimed that he was afraid something like that would happen and I had swallowed too many balloons. He said that some of them had already started to move through my digestive system.

The next thing that J-Dogg told me really screwed with my mind. He said I would have to shit out the balloons. I'm thinking "hell no! I ain't playin' in my feces!"

"You damn fool!" J-Dogg said. "That's how people get stuff in all the time." He also said they would have their people come and visit random white guys and have them pack the drugs up their asses.

J-Dogg gave me some kind of white liquid to drink and some plastic gloves. He told me not to go outside for recreation because within an hour or two I would be having a massive bowel movement. So that was how I ended up getting my first contraband in prison.

I knew that I couldn't keep using the same method because swallowing balloons was very taxing. So I had to figure out another route. There were a lot of crafty guys in prison and there was one in particular, name Tim, who I used to talk to periodically. Tim was very good at sewing so I decided to have him sew some extra pockets on the inside of my boxers. I didn't want to expose my business so I told him that the pockets were for a friend of mine who thought that he could get a better price if he went through me. Tim was a very religious brother so some things couldn't be exposed to him. But he eventually sewed my boxers to perfection. He even out a button on them to make them look normal.

Everything was going perfect. I was able to get my

weed in with no hassles and I made a shit load of money. Who needed Unicor? My room was stocked with commissary! I had every pair of shoes the Institution had to offer, plus I would buy shoes from guys coming in from other places because other prisons sold different radios and shoes. If I seen something that I liked then I had to have it.

At that time Marie was proving herself to be a rider. LaKendria was visiting often but I could tell that she was backing off a little. I didn't care because my star player was performing. Marie and I were even on planning on getting married. I used to put money on other people's books and use their pin numbers to talk to Marie. So instead of having 300 minutes a month I'd have like 900, and that wasn't even enough. I would've talked to Marie all night long if I could, but I couldn't.

Then one day after leaving from a visit with Marie a C.O. asked me if I was serious with my girlfriend. In my mind I was thinking "Hell yeah! What kind of question is that?" But I played it cool and told him that we were just friends with benefits. He then proceeded to tell me that he had seen her cuddled up with another man at the movies the night before. He said he was sure it was her because he spoke to her. And right before I came out to visit she asked him not to tell me. The C.O. said he told her that it was against prison policy. But so much for prison policy because he had just crushed my spirit!

I tried to play it cool with Marie after hearing about her being with another man. But to be honest I let my feelings get in the way of my money and my hustle. I upped the stakes on Marie and told her that I wanted her to bring me in a cell phone. It was the only way for me to keep close tabs on her. I had put my feelings back in this female and fallen for her yet again! I knew that she had slept with my partner once before so I should've known how she'd behave when I was physically unavailable.

Marie brought me the phone one day and the charger the next day. I knew that I was taking a real risk and breeching security. But, I didn't care love had me gone. My cellmate was cool with the fact that I had a phone in the cell. But I made a mistake by completely stopping my use of the regular jail phone. Prison was a very nosey place and other inmates had noticed the changes in my routine. Like I said before, them damn phones ain't straight.

My whole objective was to keep my eye on Marie. But I'll be the first person to say that nothing will stop an adult from doing what they want to do. Marie always made sure that she was accounted for during the day. But after I was asleep she had another agenda. Marie had a boyfriend who knew all about me being in prison. He would sit there quietly while her and I talked on the phone. He had plenty of time to spend with her and to work her over. I know about all of this because later on down the line when she finally broke bad on me for good she told me.

One night I was up late heating water in preparation to cook a Ramen Noodle. I had the phone up to my ear talking to one of my classmates about how he had changed his life. He told me that he had begun his own preaching ministry and before I could congratulate him there was a knock on my door. I turned around and to my surprise I was staring straight into the face of the third shift C.O.! He was more stunned to see me using a cellphone than I was to see him standing at my door without first hearing him approach. I didn't know whether I wanted to run to the toilet and try to flush the phone or to just wait for the C.O. to rush in and take it.

The C.O. had the cell door open before I could make my next move. To be honest he was calmer than I had expected for him to be. He asked me how in the hell did I get the cellphone in there. I told him that I had found it in the recreation yard. He made me turn the phone over to him and said that he'd be back later. I basically begged him not to turn me in because they might ship me off to another prison or possibly charge me with another case. The C.O. closed the door in my face.

I paced the floor all night long thinking that the Compound's Security Investigations Specialists (S.I.S.) team would be coming to get me. I told my cellmate that I was probably screwed. One hour turned into two and before I knew it shift change came without anyone coming to get me. Right before the C.O., who took my phone, was about to leave he came to my cell and told me he would let me off with only a warning. He said if he ever had any more problems out of me then he would falsify a write-up and say that I had done all kinds of things that I didn't. He asked me if I thought that was a fair deal and I said, "Hell yeah!"

But in all actuality I hadn't really learned my lesson. Not even two weeks after being busted with my first cell phone I was caught with another one. And this C.O. wasn't as nice as the first one. I was sent directly to solitary confinement to await my fate at the hands of the Disciplinary Board.

My cellmate was also taken for a ride. I was under the impression that he would take the charge since I was the one who had taken all of the risk to get the phone and he had actually used it more than I had. For those two reasons alone I assumed that he would be compassionate and let me off the hook. Well, he didn't. And he even had someone slide a note from him under my cell door asking me to take the charge because it wasn't his phone.

I ended up at a U.S.P. in Leavenworth while my cellmate got put back on the Compound at F.C.I. in Memphis. U.S.P.'s are high security Federal Prisons that consist of some of the most violent offenders in the United States of America. Leavenworth was no joke! I couldn't believe they had placed me in such a hostile environment for having a cellphone. But I found out that I would have eventually been shipped and rehoused anyway. I had a detainer for a previous Aggravated Robbery and my current charge was an armed Bank Robbery so my points and security level was high.

8

A New Set Of Rules

I could actually smell death at Leavenworth. The staff let you know immediately upon entering intake that you would be placed in the hole (segregation) for about a week to make sure you didn't have any enemies on the Compound. They ask you if you've testified against anyone and if not they allow you to enter.

Once you are in population, guys immediately ask you where you are from and if you are affiliated with any gangs or organizations. Once I told them that I was from Memphis they showed me what's called the "Dirty South Car" which is made up of all the guys from Southern States: Tennessee, Alabama, Mississippi, Florida, Carolinas, etc. They are considered your "Home-boys" and the guys from Memphis embraced me and gave me a small care package with some shower shoes, and hygiene items until my property arrived.

After all of the introductions were out of the way I was asked if I had my copy of my P.S.I. report. The homeboys in my "car" waned to read it to make sure that I hadn't snitched on anyone. In the Feds they have a golden rule; NO SNITCHES ALLOWED! They told me that if I was a snitch that I could willingly check myself into the hole and get off of the Compound and all would be well.

There was a guy named Big Head that knew me. I felt like he could pretty much vouch for my character. So I gave my P.S.I. to him personally to read. And let's just say that I ended up staying on the Compound in general population.

Big Head and I ended up cellmates and he introduced me to all of the homeboys from Memphis. There was G-Money, Tony, Fred, Top Flight, and Shorty B. I was also introduced to other members of the "Dirty South Car" but there was one person that I didn't get to meet for like a week or so. This particular person was in the hole because some "homies" from Texas were trying to extort him out of some money, which made him think that the whole "Dirty South Car" was against him. Big Head never said his name so I never asked.

Big Head gave me some very valuable advice on how to stay alive in the Feds and make it back to my family in one piece. Rule #1: Never get involved with any gambling debts. That was one of the easy ways to get stuck-on (stabbed). Rule #2: Never say anything about another man that you couldn't repeat to his face. And last but not least, Rule #3: Stay away from punks (homosexuals). These were all ways to get killed in prison. But it really didn't matter to me because none of the above was my style. And if those were the only requirements for freedom then I would definitely be seeing my family again.

One day I was in the Chow Hall when this chubby black dude approached our table.

"I'm mad at you mane!" Top Flight said to the chubby guy, "Why you check into the hole? I went through hell and hot water trying to get you out!" continued Top Flight. "Them dudes ain't bout that life Pee!"

I remember Pee responding saying "I wasn't scared of what they wanted to do to me! I was more afraid of what I had planned to do to them!"

When Pee caught eye contact with me I just nodded my head at him. But in my mind I was thinking, "Who is this cat?" Top Flight noticed my curiosity and explained to me that the chubby black dude they were calling Pee was my "homeboy" from Nashville and his name was P-Dub.

I immediately thought "This can't be the same dude that Calloway had told me about." They say never judge a book by its cover but this guy didn't look like he was worth 9 million dollars and had once tried to bribe his prosecutor into taking 15 million to let him walk away. I mean, this guy was standing in front of me with wrinkly clothes on! But it was him, indeed. I had heard so many stories about P-Dub that I was damn near star struck! There were stories about how he made all of his money and there I was in the Feds for a bank robbery where I had received $6,000 and thought that I was balling. After that first introduction, P-Dub and I didn't really say much to one another but every time I saw him I made sure that I broke my neck to speak to him.

I started to attend the Prison's Church services. I always believed in Church and God. Especially while growing up with my Pops' side of the family. They made me go to Church almost 6 days out of the week.

There was a man in Prison Church named Brother Derrick. He would always tell me that God had great things in store for me. But he said I first had to completely change my life and accept Jesus Christ as my Lord and Savior. But what I didn't want to tell Brother Derrick was that I wasn't ready to change. I was ready to learn about some of the criminal activities that were floating around in some of those prisoner's minds. I wasn't in jail to be rehabilitated; I was there because I had gotten caught. I was only in my early twenties and I felt like I had plenty of time to change.

God was truly with Bro. Derrick because this dude had healing hands. There was an incident where a guy was walking around the track on the Recreation yard. The track was around the softball diamond and there was a softball game going on at the time. The softball flew out to the track and struck the guy dead in the center of his forehead. It knocked him clean out and the cut in his head was pretty bad. He was rushed to Medical Services in secure conditions.

Now, Bro. Derrick was present that day on the softball diamond. He said to me "Juvie, God told me that he'll be alright." The Bro. Derrick just continued doing what he was doing. Later on that night before lockdown, Bro. Derrick took some prayer oil and went into the guy's room. He rubbed some of the oil around the guys wound and said a prayer. I didn't think anything of it until I saw the guy the next morning. He no longer had a head womb! And I had seen the wound with mine own eyes; it was completely gone. The man was embracing Bro. Derrick, rejoicing and saying thank you! But Bro. Derrick told the man to thank God instead. After that day people all over the prison would have Bro. Derrick pray for them, their families, and anything else they could think of.

One day while I was sitting in Prison Church, some guy came and sat down next to me. I really wasn't paying attention to who he was until the person spoke to me. He said "Juvenile I didn't think you attended Church." I looked over and the person speaking was P-Dub.

"It's cool." I responded. "We gotta get to know God and plus he shows favor in Bro. Derrick."

Right there in that Church there was a friendship made. After that day P-Dub and I began kickin' it on the Recreation Yard. I even got him to take a few jail pictures with me. And P-Dub really hated pictures.

He never asked why I was in Prison. But one day I volunteered the information hoping that it would cause him to also open up about his situations. I really wanted to know how he had gotten started and ended up so successful. But for a long time he wouldn't open up. He would make little side remarks about my case like "Damn Lil' Juvie! You too smart to be a Bank Robber!" Or to piss me off he would say, "Your petty ass robbin' banks and shit."

I remember one incident when we were out on the yard and my cellmate Big Head was trying to slick-diss (disrespect) P-Dub. Big Head was bragging about the Benz that he still had at home waiting on him for when he got out.

He even hit P-Dub with a low blow and said, "P-Dub, you got all that time you might as well let me knock your bitch off. Imma send you some pictures back and put a few dollars on your books."

P-Dub just looked at Big Head and said, "You finished? Do you really have any idea who you talkin' to? I buy my side women cars like you are driving. And them little five bricks you was copping, I don't even serve niggas nothing less than 20 at a time. If you a nigga calling me for five bricks Imma think he the police."

After that episode I guess my boy P-Dub had a point to prove. He called me to his room one day and his paperwork was spread out all over the place. He showed me how many bricks he was getting per month. 500 of them was coming out of Miami alone and another 100 from Houston. Dude was loaded!

I had all kinds of thoughts running through my head but P-Dub snapped me out of my trance.

He said, "Oh Yeah Lil' Juvie, I seen the way you looked at me in the Chow Hall the first time we met. You looked at me like I was a bum. Trust me, I pay attention to everything."

Well, I read every piece of his paperwork and it only made me crave the fast life even more. I knew that with this kind of negative influence I would get out and indulge in more crime. The more P-Dub opened up about the drug game, the more I wanted in. But, to be honest, P-Dub never wanted me to get out and commit crimes. But, he did know, I wasn't about to work for somebody else.

I knew that I wasn't about to sell cocaine. I had seen how it has affected my mom and I wanted no parts of that. So marijuana was my only and next best option.

If I was going to hustle then I should hustle big was the best advice that P-Dub gave me. He told me not to settle for anything small. He said that the smaller the quantity the bigger the chance I was taking of getting caught. I'd have to deal with petty buyers who would always come short. And if I turned them down for coming short then there was a good possibility that they'd snitch on me if they got caught.

He also told me to never sleep with any of my associate's females no matter how enticing they were. And always play fair by paying off my debts. P-Dub said, "If you owe a man a dollar then you pay him. He shouldn't have to ask you about his money. And if you are a day late in paying him then throw him some interest."

These are valuable tools that I use up to this very day. The last jewel that P-Dub gave me was on the day that I left the U.S.P. at Leavenworth. He was the last person that I had hollered at.

P-Dub said, "Juvie, go out there and stay loyal and that'll take you a long way, and one day maybe even save your life."

9

'New' Beginnings...

March 4, 2004 came relatively quick and it was my time to enter back into society. But my plan wasn't to go back to school or to get a trade. I also wouldn't be slaving at someone's warehouse with the possibility of being laid off when business slows up. My mission was clear: I wanted a quick come-up and I had learned in the penitentiary that I didn't need a gun and a mask in order to make it happen.

I know that I had the gift of gab and the ability to get people to do the things that I needed them to do. But I needed to put my ear to the streets in order to find out what type of criminal activity I would apply myself to.

My female friend, Tay, picked me up at the prison gate. She rolled me around for a while to shoot the breeze with my family members and associates. I told her that I needed to make some cash because I needed some clothes, a car, and my own place to stay. So she told me about what she had going on with income taxes.

I had gotten out like a month before income tax season was about to end. Tay filled me in on a side hustle she would do every year. By preparing and filing people's taxes for them she would make a decent income for herself. She said that everyone was out their doing taxes, scamming the I.R.S. by filing bogus tax returns in other people's names and setting up business accounts so the money could be direct deposited. She said that the victim's of the income tax fraud would still get their return but it would just be a long and drawn out process.

I remember thinking that the information was irrelevant because whatever Tay had going on had nothing to do with me. Why would she enlighten me on something that I couldn't benefit from? But, I kept these thoughts to myself.

I ended up moving in with my sister Lee Lee and her five children. She was still coupled-up with my ex-weed supplier who had fathered her two youngest daughters, my nieces. We all crammed into Lee Lee's two-bedroom apartment in the Raleigh's Springs Apartments on James Road.

I really enjoyed being back around my family, especially my nieces and nephews. My sister and I had always been close. My mother had always made sure that we hung out together when we were young and we maintained that relationship into our adulthood.

Lee Lee always tried to keep me on the right track. And she made sure to let me know that although she didn't have much, whatever she did have was mine. That's the way that it always has been and it always will be.

Lee Lee told me that a lot of things had changed within the few years of my absence. My mom had started hanging back out at Tee's house. I couldn't believe she would go back there after knowing what Tee had done to me. I mean she helped the system send me to prison! Also, Marie and her boyfriend had moved in together. Even though I had vowed to never mess around again, my plan was to destroy her happy little home.

Even though I was welcome at Lee Lee's house, I knew I wasn't about to shack up there. I needed a place of my own so I had to find some unassuming female victims who'd let me shack up in their crib while I got my shit together. I love my sister but I was out of there.

April was a prime suspect. She used to write me periodically towards the end of my prison stint. And now she was going through a divorce with her husband. But the fact that she was married and had three children wouldn't allow me to take our situation serious.

Meanwhile I had started hanging back in the streets with Lil' Black and Goldmouth. We would always try to find some females to scheme up on. Especially Lil' Black, he loved playing women out of their money so he was my perfect partner in crime.

One day I was sitting on Lee Lee's front porch just enjoying the weather. The ice cream truck was perusing the neighborhood and its bell could be heard for blocks, enticing all of the children to come and make their selections. Children came running from everywhere and I myself decided to have some ice cream on that hot day also.

As I walked up to the truck preparing to place my order, I heard someone behind me say, "You should be ashamed of yourself! Skippin' all 'dem kids!"

When I turned around to curse the person out for getting in my business I was surprised to see a pretty lady. I was like "Damn!" Uh...my bad. And your name is?"

"Tricey," the women said. "Now move and let these children through!"

"Only if you give me your number," I replied.

I never did get my ice cream that day, but I did get Tricey's number. We began having phone conversations immediately. Tricey said she didn't normally invite people over to her house but I seemed cool. Plus, she said that she knew Lee Lee because she used to live in the same apartment building as her.

I went over to Tricey's house later on that night. She cooked a meal and introduced me to her four children: Keon, Kierra, Lil' Tommy, and Tamara. These children were well mannered and respectful. Lil' Tommy stood out to me more than the other three. He was only five years old but he had a solidly built frame as if he was a body builder.

I remember telling Lil' Tommy that he was too young to workout and I asked him how be had gotten that way. Lil' Tommy told me that he did workout and that he could do 100 pushups straight and I could count them to make sure that he had done them all. And trust me, this little dude was a beast! He seemed like he had already been on this planet before in another lifetime. He talked to me like he was grown but always with respect.

I warmed up to Tricey. I didn't want to misuse her because she trusted me. She let me use her car whenever I wanted and she allowed me to be around her children. In no time, we were all living under the same roof. Now, I had yet to find and secure a steady income. But that would change after hooking back up with my mom. One day my phone rung and it was mom on the other end.

"Hey baby!" Mom said. "You done been out the Feds for some time now and I still haven't seen my oldest baby yet."

I was still a little upset because she was hanging with the enemy but I couldn't tell her that so I just played it cool.

"Mom, I was coming to see you. I was first trying to get myself together so I could have something for you when I come," I responded.

Mom never asked her for anything. But. I still wanted to give her something just for giving me life and being there for me whenever she could. I asked her where she was located and she told me that she was over Tee's house (it figures). I wanted to tell her that I wasn't going anywhere near Tee's house but I went and saw my mom anyway.

I felt so awkward being back inside the house where I had acquired so many evil memories. But I hunkered down and made it through. And right before I left my mother spoke to me and said, "Look baby, I ain't really got a lot to offer you right now and your sister told me that you moved out and got you a little family and all. Here, see if you can do something with this."

She pulled out four -100 dollar bills, four - 50 dollar bills, and five - 20 dollar bills. When she tried to hand me the money I refused.

"Naw mom, I can't take your money. I'll survive," I said.

"Take it. It ain't real no way, it's counterfeit," mom responded.

My eyes got as big as golf balls.

"How'd you get this, mom?" I asked. "I wanted all of

it. I can do plenty with this!"

"I made it myself," mom said. "I sell this as a side hustle."

Right then and there my new hustle was formed. Eventually I put a team together consisting of Parris, Bar Bar, Lil' Black, and Goldmouth. When I showed them the counterfeit money and asked them what could we do with it, they pretty much all responded in unison as if they had rehearsed their answer. They all said we could sell it for wholesale prices.

But I didn't want to sell it. I had other things in mind, like: buying product from local dope boys; buying me a new wardrobe; or, looking through the Auto-Trader magazine and finding a vulnerable car seller whom I could finesse out of a car and title. But first I needed mom to tell me everything what I needed to know about making my own counterfeit money and where to get all of the materials. Once she told me everything could be purchased at Office Max, that place became my second home.

My next move was to scrape up all of the money that I needed in order to purchase the supplies for my counterfeiting operation. So I figured I'd get mom to give whatever she could spare and I'd somehow exchange it for legal currency. I started out with $2,000 including the $700.00 mom had given me when we first reunited. My only mission was to get the money exchanged fast without getting caught.

My first target was the local newspaper company. I used fraudulent $20.00 bills to produce $2.00 papers and received $18.00 worth of real currency in return. We figured that the newspapers would be easy targets because on Sundays they used children between the ages of 13-16. It was only a one-shot deal because once the boss got a hold of our fake bills and realized that he had been duped he would probably put more experienced people out on the paper route.

The team split up in order to cover more area. Bar Bar went to Raleigh, Parris went to North Memphis, and Goldmouth, Lil' Black, and myself covered East Memphis, South Memphis, and the White Haven area. We were very successful.

We started off with a small Lexmark 3 and 1 copying machine and some 25% all white copying paper, which allowed us to print up more fake bills and pull-off bigger schemes. Our next target was Cornerstones. We damn near terrorized every store Frayer, Raleigh, North Memphis, and Millington. I had gotten so obsessed with how easy the hustle was that I had began stressing the point that our job wasn't done until one of our bills was posted on the counter of every Cornerstone with black markings revealing its fraudulence. And once that happened I knew that we had to relocate our operation elsewhere.

One day while we were out grinding (hustling) I got a call from Lee Lee informing me that a U.S. Treasury check had come in the mail with my name on it. I thought that it was a joke or some kind of a scam but I went and picked it up anyway. When I opened it up and saw how much it was worth I got seriously pissed off.

The last federal institution that I was in had sent my info to the United State Treasury department. They in return forwarded to me the money that I had on my books upon release, which was a $.02 check.

Right then a light bulb came on in my head. If I could

find the right person to alter the balance on the check, then we could cash it for a much longer amount. I knew the right person to call was my friend Tay since she was in the tax business. I figured since Tay dealt with people's I.D.s, social security cards, and birth certificates all day long she would probably know how to either alter the check herself or at least point me in the right direction toward somebody who could. And I was right because a few days later I walked out of the Harrah's Casino in Tunica, Mississippi with a little under $10,000.00 in cash. And boy was that a big mistake!

I'd never had that much money to call my own before. I had enough money to buy me the Hewlett Packard 3 and 1 printer that I really wanted and to upgrade my paper to a 75% cotton grade. I also bought a car and some fresh gear (clothes) so that I could look up to par. In the end I had everything that I needed to continue my counterfeit operation.

Another hustle that I put into effect was charming females that worked the cash registers at Old Navy and Kohl's. I would convince them to allow me to fill up baskets full of clothes and they would pretend as if they rung everything up at the register. In return I would get them whatever clothes they wanted for their children.

This new scheme was easy. But eventually the females at both jobs began to get greedy. It got to the point where they would already have all of the clothes they wanted PLUS any new arrivals of men's clothing I didn't already have put to the side. That way all that I had to do was walk into the store, fill up the basket with the clothes that the girls had reserved and just wait for the perfect opportunity to push the basket right out the front door.

From there I ended up propositioning other females

in different stores. Some of them agreed but some of them were scared. For the scared ones, I would use the incentive of a fake $100 bill. The fact that they were nervous caused them to neglect the careful scrutiny needed to detect fraudulent money. If I couldn't get clothes I would trick them into changing out my fake cash for legit tender so either way their register still came up short at the end of their shift.

My counterfeit operation had taken off better than I had expected. We were showing up all over the place and slipping businesses fake bills. We didn't spare anyone! We went from the Mid South Fair to Fire Work City, during the fourth of July holiday, to the Memphis State Tigers football and basketball concession stands. Anybody whom we felt was an easy mark would get got.

One day Parris found some people who wanted to sell us seven pounds of marijuana over in West Memphis, Arkansas. It was supposed to be a smooth exchange. We would give them $1,000 for each pound and they would give us the marijuana. The only problem was that they didn't know our money was fake.

We showed in two cars because we didn't trust those country boys one bit. And when we got there the dealer had a change of plan. He now wanted one of us to come inside and weigh up the weed while he counted the money to make sure that the dal went smoothly.

Parris decided to be the one who'd go inside to make the deal. I didn't think it was a good idea because although the money looked and felt real to the touch someone who knew what to look for could spot the inaccuracies. And after being in the house for about five minutes tops I heard Pow! Pow! Pow! and Parris came running out with a bag in his hand. We escaped that incident with our lives and no one was physically harmed.

Two weeks after the West Memphis incident I got a disturbing call from Lee Lee. She said that two United States Secret Service Agents had come by the house and requested to speak with me. The Agents said they had something to discuss with me and that it was urgent for me to give them a call. Talk about somebody having bubble guts! What the hell did the President's bodyguards need to speak with me about?

I had Lee Lee give me the Agent's name and number. And when I called the guy he knew exactly who I was as if we were childhood friends or something. We scheduled a meeting for the following Friday at 10:00 a.m. at the First Tennessee Bank on Poplar Street. I remember thinking "Why in the world would we be meeting at a bank?"

When the day came I took Lil' Black and my cousin Kee Kee with me. I figured that it couldn't be that serious since we were meeting in a public place. But once we were inside the bank entrance we were buzzed into a separate building apart from where the banking activity took place. There was a receptionist at a front desk and a sign that read U.S. Service Office.

Once the interview began the Agents got straight to the point.

"You're here because you cashed a U.S. Treasury check at the Harrah's Casino in the Northern District of Mississippi. We have your face on surveillance camera from every angle of the Casino. We have you walking in to the Casino, up to the cash register, and back out again. You will be indicted here in the near future. Do you have any additional States that you want to add by helping yourself?" the Agents explained to me.

I told the agents that I had no idea as to what they were referring to. The agent became pissed off and said, "Cut the bullshit! I can tell you ain't too bright Kendrick because you've got the nerves to walk up in here with your two lil' buddies that was at the casino with you that night!"

I was rendered speechless and there was a few seconds of complete silence. I was thinking about how big of a mistake was made. I was too greedy. I walked into the Casino and cashed that check myself. I would have been better off if I'd had found a mule, bought them some fake I.D., and had them cash it for me.

The agent broke the ice and said "What? Cat got your tongue?"

"If you've got me than you've got me," I replied.

All I kept thinking was that I was headed back to the Federal Penitentiary. I hadn't even been out for a whole year yet. And just as I was about to walk out of the door the shorter Agent amongst the bunch spoke up.

"Oh yeah, Kendrick I almost forgot. We know all about your little counterfeit ring, too. We just got a call about that this morning right before you got here," the Agent said.

I wondered how someone would know to call the Secret Service about me selling counterfeit instead of the usual Crime Stoppers hotline? I was reminded later that I had used Aunt Tee's address as my home address when I did my P.S.I. in prison. So that was the first place that the Secret Service went before they showed up at Lee's Lee's house. Damn! Aunt Tee had sent the authorities at me again! This lady had some serious hate for me.

My counterfeit ring eventually came to an end with me being indicted in both the Northern District of Mississippi for check fraud and the Western District of Tennessee for counterfeit. My run had come to an end. The game was over. I had caught three Federal cases in a short period of time and the Feds operate according to guidelines surrounding your past criminal history, amongst other things. So there was a good possibility that they would dub me a career Criminal.

My first order of business was to head down to Oxford, Mississippi and face the unthinkable. I knew that the racist rebel flag was highly revered by a healthy number of the Oxford population. Therefore, my chances of receiving any mercy were slim. But luckily I ended up being represented by a decent Public Defender who believed in ethics and fairness.

After sitting in the Oxford Jail for six months, I went ahead and signed a plea agreement for 10 months jail time and three years on supervised release. But once I was back in Memphis I knew that I had a much harder fight because I was facing two sentences: one for the counterfeit and the other for violating my supervised release. I called my Probation Officer and he was cool, calm, and collected. He told me that I'd be fine because it was only a White Collar crime and so the guidelines weren't too bad.

I was feeling really optimistic because my lawyer and I were on the same page. Then they ended up appointing me a new Public Defender, and I felt like that change could have possibly worked out for my benefit. But, the initial meeting with the new Attorney didn't go as well as I expected. He was very pessimistic and talked about consecutive sentences and the possibility of me doing more time than I did on my Bank Robbery conviction.

I encourage any and everybody to do their own personal research if they ever end up facing Federal charges for whatever situation. The reason why is because these Public Defenders go to school for all of those years to get their law degrees and most of them come out without a clue about the way the Federal guidelines actually work. Now, this doesn't apply to all of the seasoned veteran Public Defenders who actually put forth an honest effort to study each individual case that comes across their desk with the intent to get their client the fairest sentence possible. Also, remember that 95% of your sentence will be determined according to your P.S.I. report.

To make a long story short, I fired the new Attorney and hired a paid Attorney. The paid Attorney informed me about some new laws that had been passed giving Federal Judges more power over the sentencing of offenders. For instances, if a person has a sentencing range of 41-51 months but the Judge feels like your crime is severe enough to merit a harsher penalty, then he or she could sentence you above the maximum (51 months) of your sentencing guidelines. It also worked the opposite; you could be sentenced beneath your minimum.

The new laws had both pros and cons depending on which Courtroom you were in and what Judge you had. There were three Federal Judges for the Western District of Tennessee: John P. McCalla, Judy Givens, and Bernice Donald.

The Judge who presided over my Bank Robbery case was Judge McCalla. McCalla had a bad habit of telling offenders if he could give them more time than what their guidelines allowed then he would. There was another female Judge whom I personally saw break some of the toughest dudes in the city and send them back from court in tears.

She didn't care if your mother was in the courtroom on her deathbed; she spared none. This lady stuck to whatever the Government recommended. And last but not least there was the fairest judge that I had ever had the opportunity to come cross. This third Judge didn't roll with either side even though she was limited by Federal guidelines. It was pleasure to encounter her and to this day, I feel like I let her down more than my family and myself.

Due to the fact that my Probation Officer and I were on good terms and both of my cases had ended up in the fairest courtroom I felt like my chances were pretty good; or so I thought. The day of my Violation Hearing my P.O. flipped the script on me! He sounded like a rehearsed Prosecutor, saying that I needed to be put away for at least five years. What! I was confounded! The guidelines for my violation were only four to 10 months.

I immediately raised my hand to speak. "Your honor, that ain't what he told me! When he and I talked on the phone he said that he would ask for leniency. This is a totally different person that's speaking before you today. Plus, I've already been in custody for 11 months," I said.

I ended up getting time served for my probation violation and being placed on supervised house arrest for another 11 months. I was also given 11 months jail credit for the time that I had served in Mississippi. Boy was I a happy camper! I was going to be at home a couple of days after Christmas and definitely before New Years.

10

Same Ole', Same Ole'

But, I still hadn't learned my lesson. My only concern was to get back into the swing of things, quick! I was broke with no money and Tricey and I had split up. I won't say she didn't hold me down while I was away. She did the best she could with what she had. But I did suspect some things I couldn't prove, so I figured that it would be best for us to go our separate ways. So I ended up back on my sister's couch, once again.

I hooked back up with April whose divorce from her husband was final. And I also hooked up with one of my childhood girlfriends named Big Baby. Through it all these females had been there for me whenever I needed them the most.

My attempts to keep April and Big Bay from knowing about one another didn't work. April's cousin worked at the same place as Big Baby and one day I had become the topic of their conversation. Damn! Small world!

I went to visit my old P.O. in order to find out who my new P.O. was and to get the house arrest ankle monitor placed on my leg. I couldn't believe how blunt my Old P.O. was! He made it no secret that he wasn't too happy about me being free.

"Well, if it ain't the luckiest man alive! You're the first person I ever seen get off that easy. Some Judges shouldn't even be in their active positions. I don't believe she would have let you off if you would have killed somebody," he said.

I just sat there staring at him and thinking, "Where has this dudes professionalism went."

He eventually introduced me to my new P.O. and the guy was a nightmare. It was obvious they had been talking to one another about me. I knew that I wasn't going to like the new P.O. because all he talked about was my past crimes. I thought the P.O.'s job was to make sure the people assigned to his caseload were being productive citizens of society and meeting all of the conditions and requirements of their probation. If a crime is committed by an assignee then there job was to violate them. And it's as simple as that.

No matter what my P.O. said, I was going to get me some fast money whether he liked it or not. I had gotten released just in time for the 2006 tax season. Plus, Tay and I had remained in contact. So my plan was to find any and everybody that I could who needed their taxes prepared and send them to Tay. In return, I would get a $5,000.00 cut.

The problem was, I was on house arrest and couldn't move around freely. The only thing I was allowed to do was go to work and then back home. But I figured that it was easy to get around that problem. All I had to do was to get an under the table job that would say that I worked their when I really didn't But I would still have to hang around the job site because my P.O. told me that when I did get a job he would just periodically pop-up without calling to warn me beforehand. And if I wasn't at work he'd violate me immediately and make sure that I'd go back to prison. So I had to think quickly.

The solution came to me in the blink of an eye. I

remembered Big Baby telling me that her uncle had just recently gotten out of prison and that he was currently working at one of his partner's businesses. So I called her and asked if her uncle could put me in a position to look like I was working the job. I told her that it didn't matter whether they paid me or not I just needed it to look real to keep my P.O. satisfied while I hustled with the tax situation on the side. She told me that she was pretty sure he could help me and she wanted to introduce me to her uncle, J.T., because she felt like he and I had a lot in common. I really wasn't interested in meeting her uncle but I needed his help so I agreed.

For a dude just getting out of prison, J.T. had his priorities straight. He was married, had a nice 6 figure home in South Haven, MS, had a few nice cars, and A-1 credit. I was really digging dude's style plus he was much older than me with a laid back demeanor.

J.T. and I kicked it off good and he introduced me to his partner Nic. Nic was the owner of "Bob's Market" off of Whitney Avenue and Overton Crossing in the Frayser area. Nic had agreed to give me a job or to make it look like I had worked in his place of business. All I had to do was to send my P.O. his way and he would confirm my employment.

My P.O. came to check the place out and immediately gave me his opinion. He didn't think it would be a good idea for me to work at Bob's Market because it was located in a high crime and drug infested area. I told him that I wasn't there to sell drugs; I was there to work and make money. He eventually agreed to allow me to work there but said that he would feel more comfortable if I found something better. He reminded me of the white guy in the movie "Menace II Society" because he was scared to come around the black neighborhood after dark, which was good for me because I wouldn't have to worry about him popping up on me after certain hours.

My original intentions weren't to actually work the job. But once I started going in from 8 a.m. – 10 a.m. and helping Nic around the place I eventually began to enjoy it. But before I could completely commit I had to make my money from the tax deals on the side.

I came up with a plan: I would spend more time at Bob's Market, recruit as many of his customers as I could and send them to my partner Tay to have their taxes prepared. In the year of 2006 alone I pulled in about $30,000. I even figured out how to do some taxes on my own and it worked out to my benefit.

Nic and I had ended up getting pretty tight. He would let me work in the shop with his cousin, Abdul. As time went on they started trusting me to work the cash register and to close the place up at night by myself. These dudes were Arabs embracing an African American as their own. I couldn't thank J.T. enough. My experience with them prepared me to run my own business.

Abdul schooled me about what most Iranian men thought about us African American men. He said they weren't too fond of us because we were reckless with the way we handled our business, and too flashy. They tolerated us and accepted our money because we are big spenders and they love sleeping with our black women. They say that we don't know how to treat our black women.

Although Abdul never held any punches, I don't believe he was a racist. He invited me over to his house plenty of times. We would close up the store at 7 p.m. I had to be at home by 9 p.m. or else the U.S. Marshalls would be looking for me all over the place. So I would have a few hours to mess off. I had already made up my mind that if ever a time came when I couldn't make it home, in time, I would just cut off my ankle monitor.

Abdul's woman and son were usually present when I came over. He would normally cook us on Arabic dish and he'd sit back and sip on some Henny and coke. My first time tasting Hennessey and Coca-Cola was with Abdul and I've been hooked every since. Abdul and I shared a drink from the same cup often.

I blew through the whole $30,000 that I had made that year during tax season. I bought a couple of cars, upgraded my wardrobe, and purchased a few other things. I ended up right back at square one; broke.

My strained financial situation caused me to go backwards. I hooked up with one of my associates who liked to go out and snatch cash registers from businesses during regular operating hours. I mean this dude would actually get in line at a store and once it was his turn to be rung up he would snatch the whole cash register and break out the door running. All he wanted me to do was to go into particular places and let him know how many people were working, how many cameras there were, and if there were any security guards inside. If everything went well he would split the drawer with me.

Everything went smoothly with the Robberies. But I knew that I was playing Russian roulette with my freedom. I was on Federal house arrest and I knew that if I was connected to the Robberies in any kind of way then I was done far. So I fell all the way back from those suicide missions rather quickly.

By the time the 2007 tax season came around everything was working out for me. I made more money than I had ever counted in my life, at the time. I had basically tripled my amount from the previous year.

Nic offered to sub-lease the store to me because he was growing tired of the business and wanted to pursue other things. So we settled on a decent amount and I was in business. I never informed my P.O. about the change. I kept everything the same way because I figured that everything was running okay and if it ain't broke, then don't try to fix it.

I began to do things differently as far as management goes. I would have all kinds of store give-a-ways in order to bring more customers through the door. I met all kinds of new people.

Since the store was officially in my possession I would sit around the shop and drink until it was time for me to make my 9 p.m. curfew. There was one particular guy that I met, named Highway, who would come to the store often and hangout with my guys and me. This dude eventually helped me to take my hustle to a whole new level.

One day while we were hanging around the shop the subject of drugs became our topic. Highway told me that he used to sell cocaine by the kilo. Although I listened to him I wasn't really interested in selling cocaine. But his next subject caught my attention. He said that he had a marijuana plug in Houston, Texas that was just waiting for him to make the move and go out there. It sounded like a proposition.

This was the opportunity that I had been waiting for. I took a couple of days to think it over. A lot of things had played inside my head from past conversations I had with P-Dub in the Feds. His advice to me was that whatever I decided to do in life, I should always do it big.

I knew that messing around in the drug trade came with its own risks. What if we get caught? Plus, I didn't really know this dude Highway too well. And if I decided to take on this endeavor, how would we get the weed back to Tennessee?

At the end of my self-deliberation process, I was like fuck it. I didn't have anything to lose. But if everything went well, I had everything to gain.

I hit up Highway and let him know that I was down. I told him that I wanted to start off by purchasing 20 pounds. I wanted him to find out how much that costs and to get back with me.

Highway made the call and got back with me a little while later. He said there were two different prices because there were two different kinds of weed called "Reggie" which is a name for mid-level grade marijuana. One was light green with big stalks of bud and the other one was small buds with no seeds called "Popcorn" because of its resemblance to microwave popcorn. Highway's Source told us to just come because by the time we got there it was likely that he might have a different kind of marijuana. Weed is plentiful in Texas so no one is committed to holding on to the product so they deal on a first come, first service basis. So, I put together $15,000 to get me what I needed and to furnish our trip.

Highway had earned his name honestly. He didn't mind riding on the highways and he mostly liked to ride by himself and watch out the best that he could for the K-9 teams and highway patrolmen posted up on the side of the highways in hidden areas. He explained to me that the K-9 teams were mostly the biggest threats because they are trained to watch out for drug traffickers by looking for trails.

Most drug traffickers ride in pairs. The car that is in the front will be speeding, If a highway patrolman is out he will pull over the speeding car while the car in the back with the narcotics will pass on by.

There have been times where the decoy has been pulled over and the driver was found to have a petty warrant for an unpaid ticket, child support, or a suspended license, and they squealed in order to avoid going to jail out of State. But sometimes you can still slip past a lazy or inexperienced patrolman. But the K-9 team is totally different.

The highway patrol's K-9 team is not only trained to watch for car tailing but they also spot-check for certain license plates from different states. Let's say for instance there is a car coming out of Texas on I-10 with Florida, Tennessee, or North Carolina plates, just to name a few. They are likely to be pulled over for any made up reason. On the highway the law enforcement don't play by the rules.

It seems like all of the laws go out the window with the K-9 team. You can have everything legit from your license, insurance, and registration. But once they run the K-9 around your vehicle and they hit on a detection of narcotics, they no longer need your consent to search the vehicle. In all actuality, they are going to search anyway. If they find you in possession of contraband you're done. Normally these stops turn up empty and after tearing up your car. They'll send you on your way.

Highway and I set a date for when we would be leaving. I got all of my affairs in order and brought along one of my partners named Big Nose to make the 9-hour ride with us. Once we arrived in Texas, I was both excited and nervous at the same time. Nervous because I wanted this transition to run smoothly and excited because I was about to have me a plug on the weed. Plus, I loved the way the city looked! I would advise anyone who has never been to Houston to visit there at least once in his or her lifetime.

Highway gave his Source the confirmation that we had hit the city. He told him that we were going to get something to eat and then check into a hotel. The Source gave us a few hotel ideas that were on the North side of the city. One of the hotels was the Sunset Inn off Basinett Street. He said it would be a good place to stay since we would be meeting up with him later on that side of town once we were comfortably settled in.

We found our hotel location and purchased a room. Then, in order to kill some time we hit the Green Pointe Mall and did a little shopping. We mingled around until it was time to get down to business.

Highway's Source was to meet us at the hotel and show us a couple of samples of what he had. Highway introduced me as his partner and said he wanted to do everything in front of me so that all of the business would be handled straight up and down. The Source introduced himself as Big Tee. Now, I finally had a name and face to put with the voice that I had been hearing on the other end of the phone.

Highway took a sample from each one of the marijuana plants. He couldn't tell which one he liked the best because both strands were worth buying. So, he rolled a blunt of each for him and Big Nose to smoke in order to make the best decision.

I can remember that the price had dropped on one and went up on the other. Highway felt that the prices were decent. For the lower grade, Big Tee wanted $435.00 a pound, which put me at $8,700. For the "Popcorn," he wanted $525.00 a pound, which would have out me at $10,500. I would have bought either one but after Highway and Big Nose smoked both blunts we decided to pay $435.00 a pound because they said that it hit hard and had a fruity taste.

After we conducted our business with Big Tee we said our goodbyes and promised to get right back at him. Next, we had to prepare our exit route for the next day. We had to get all of our materials so that we could mail the weed back to Tennessee. We were going to use the interstate and do the car-tailing trick but since it was only 20 pounds and we wanted to save on costs like gas and extra mouths to feed, we just agreed to send it through the mail. All we needed was an address to send it to, and that was the easy part.

Highway showed me how to conceal the marijuana. We went to Home Depot and purchased a small point bucket, some tape, some boxes, and a box cutter. Then we went to Wal-Mart and purchased pepper, fabric softener, and saran wrap. We took all of our supplies back to the hotel and did our business. We took the packages to the nearest U.P.S. and overnight shipped them with a tracking number. If all went well the package would be there in 24 hours.

After shipping the package off, we got some breakfast and hit the interstate to go home. Once we completed our long exhausted trip back to Memphis we all went our separate ways. We promised to meet up at "Bob's Market" by 8 a.m. in order to case the area where the package was designated to land.

Everything went according to the plan and I officially received my first drug shipment. I was happier than a kid in a candy factor! Highway took me to Wal-Mart and showed me what kind of digital scale to buy and what type of Ziploc bags we would use once the pounds were broken down. The last thing he did was show me how to set the digital scale in order to properly weigh the pounds. Everything else was easy.

Highway explained to me that the kind of weed we had, could be sold for $1,000 a pound. But I told him to give me $900 a pound and he said that he was cool with the $100 profit. I can remember wondering why he was keeping it so real with me (or so I thought).

Highway made a few calls and literally had the weed gone in less than 2 hours. I made a hell of a profit! I was ready to do a U-turn back to Texas and order up 40 pounds!

We waited a few days and placed another call in to Big Tee. We told him that everything was good and asked him what kind of weed was he currently selling. We told him that if he had the same kind then we wanted to purchase double the amount of the first batch. Big Tee told us that he would get up with his people and then get back with us.

Highway's phone was jumping! The same few people who had bought the 20 pounds wanted some more. A few of the guys even claimed they refused to spend their money with anyone other than Highway. I learned later on down the line, this was just a sales pitch to get the dealer to hurry up and get some more product, but in all actuality there aren't too many dealers that will hold on to their money and wait for one supplier, even if the product was good. They would move on to the next distributor to ensure that their phone continued to ring with customers.

A week went by without us hearing from Big Tee, I got impatient and asked Highway what was up with his guy. Did he forget about us? But Highway advised me to remain patient because Big Tee wanted to make a profit off of us just as bad as we wanted to make our money in return.

We finally got the call from Big Tee telling us that his people had gotten everything straight with the product. He said that we needed to move fast because they had a strand of marijuana that was light green with orange hairs and people were coming from all over the place to grab this new batch. Highway tried to explain to me all about the difference of orange hairs and purple hairs, etc. but I couldn't understand it because I didn't smoke it. I thought weed was weed.

We ended up riding back to Texas. Since we were purchasing double our first amount we decided to use the car-tailing trick. We arrived and called Big Tee to let him know that we made it to town. We grabbed a bite to eat and checked into the same hotel.

The hotel parking lot had a bunch of different cars in the lot with Tennessee license plates. Some dudes were standing around outside smoking weed and one them with cornrows in his head asked us where we were from. When Highway spoke up and told him that we were from Memphis the dude said he was also. He said there were plenty of Memphis guys staying in the same hotel and that they were pimping. They brought women to Texas to strip at clubs and to work off of "Backpage." A lot of the time they would be out until 6 a.m.

The guy eventually introduced himself as Pimp. We kinda warmed up to him a little and let him know that we were in town to score some green. He informed us that he had a dude that he bought his weed from to smoke on while he's in the club. He said the supplier would transport the marijuana to you. We told Pimp that we'd keep him in mind in case we ever needed him. I didn't want to mess up the good thing that I had going with Big Tee. We exchanged numbers with Pimp and promised him we'd come by the strip club and hang out.

Big Tee finally pulled up on us. He brought the whole 40 pounds and a big ass digital scale! He told us that he had to charge us an extra 20 cents this time because the last time he gave it to us at the same ticket price that he paid. I was super pissed! I just didn't show it.

Luckily I had brought about $25,000 with me on that trip. The 20 cents meant 20 extra dollars added to the price of each pound. I could have sworn that Highway told me that the ticket would be the same as the last time. But after Big Tee saw how excited Highway and Big Nose was about the look, texture, and taste then all of a sudden the price went up. I took a mental note in the back of my head to use the same move to my advantage in the future. I know that they say "the game is meant to be sold, not told" but I figured its only game when you keep it to yourself and it becomes common knowledge when you tell it to somebody else.

I paid the price and business went just as well as the first time. When we got back to Memphis the 40 pounds was gone within days. Big Nose had found himself some customers as well, so all of us profited off of the package.

I kept on living at my sister's house and by that time she had moved into a 3-bedroom home. I had enough money to move in to my own place but my P.O. was so nosey that it was a risk that I couldn't afford. I was running circles around my P.O.!

Once I was done with my 11 months home confinement, I was basically a loose canon and money was my canon call. The more money I made, the more I kept spending. I was blowing money fast but I was picking up a new trade in the process. J.T. had put me up on the credit game and told me he was into Real Estate. He said that he thought Real Estate would be a lucrative move for me and that I should try to acquire as many houses as I could and sit on them during the recession.

I bought one property and allowed Tricey and her 4 children to move in. Although her and I were no longer an item, I still had love for her, and I appreciated her for welcoming me as a complete stranger into her home upon my release from the Feds. Plus, she was doing me a favor because by making monthly payments on the mortgage it showed good standings on my credit.

I also bought a lot of vehicles with good bodily conditions but probably needed some engine work done. I would find decent motors and transmissions at the junkyard, put them into the cars, and slap "for sale signs" on the vehicles. I would even allow customers to make monthly payments. The car business was slow but it served the purpose of bringing in some legitimate income and boosted my credit to where I needed it to be in order to handle my future endeavors. I had cash flowing in from "Bob's Market," car sales, and my illegal drug operations.

11

All Good Things Must Come to An End

One day we had just pulled in from Houston with a 50-pound buy and everyone was exhausted from the trip. April and I had still been messing around a little and so I had keys to her house, in Raleigh, which was only a 3 minute drive from my sister's house where I live. April was at work so I went and dropped the contraband off at her house. I planned on going back to get it before she and her children got home by 5 p.m. I put the luggage in her bedroom closet, locked her door and went home to get some much needed rest.

I over slept and was awakened by a phone call a little after 5 p.m. that evening. April was on the other end of the phone screaming that someone had broken into her home. I didn't know what the hell she was talking about but I told her not to call the police and that I'd be there in less than 5 minutes.

Once I arrived I questioned her about how they had gotten in. April said the intruder had climbed in through her bedroom window. I was thinking in my mind about how someone would know that I had brought the package to April's house when it was a last minute decision on my part?

I walked into April's room and looked for the luggage in the closet. To my surprise it was still there! I opened it up and discovered that it had been untouched. The clowns had broken in without knowing exactly what they were looking for and so they took the Xbox and T.V. instead. I paid for April's window and we never reported the incident.

In the spring of 2008 one of my children's mother and I went to one of my favorite restaurants in the city called "Best Wings of Memphis" on Summer Avenue. They had some of the best fried catfish and banana pudding. I told my child's mom to grab me a couple of banana puddings from out of cooler and I heard a female's voice say,
"Girl don't be lettin' him boss you around like that."

I looked towards the cash register to see who it was that was in my business like that. The site of this woman blew me away! She reminded me of the actress Lisa Raye off of the movie, The Players Club." Now, don't get me wrong, the woman I was with was also a beauty but we were having problems at the time because she had aborted our baby before we had the chance to discuss it.

I told the woman that she needed to mind her own business. My ole' lady and her greeted one another and expressed how they hadn't seen each other in a long time. I was really bummed out that they knew each other because I wanted to get this new woman on my team.

Once my woman and I got back to the car I was about to bring up the subject about how rude the woman in the restaurant was. But before I could my ole' lady explained to me that she used to be involved with the woman's brother and that the woman's name was LaRaye. She said that LaRaye's father owned "Best Wings". I made a mental note to take her with me the next time I went to get some banana pudding.

A few days later I had stopped at the liquor store

right across the street from the "Best Wings' Restaurant to get me a pint of Hennessey. I looked across the street and saw LaRaye getting out of a Charger and going in for work. I pulled across the street, sat in the parking lot and downed my whole pint of cognac. And boy was I feeling myself! I was dressed to kill, my pockets were on swole, and I felt like I could charm any female in the world.

I counted to 3 and got out of the car. I walked in grabbed 2 banana puddings and proceeded to the counter. Once LaRaye and I had gotten face to face I said, "That was real cute how you got in my business the other day."

"What you talkin' bout?" replied LaRaye.

I told her not to worry about it but that she needed to be writing my number down and calling me as soon as she got out of work. I told her, if she didn't I was going to harass her until she put a stalking charge on me.

She responded by telling me that it would be easy to do because her boyfriend was a police officer. She said that since I was so arrogant and cute she would take my number and see what's up.

I thought that she felt like I was playing so I reached across the counter and grabbed her arm and said "Naw, you gone call me when you get off and your police friend is gonna be mad at you tonight because you are gonna be mine." I left out of there feeling like I had made my point.

I went back to my store because there was a dude who needed to talk to me about some weed that he had bought from me a while back. The shit kind of threw me for a loop because at that time I wasn't dealing directly with customers.

Once I arrived at the store there was a dude parked beside my store in a dark blue Grand AM. He got out of his car, approached my driver side window, and said, "Say bruh, I come with respect. You don't know me but I heard a lot of stuff about you. I have been buying a couple of P's from ya'll through another dude and he been bussin' my head on the ticket. Plus, I bought them last joints from ya'll and they was a lil' seedy."

I stopped him and said, "What the hell you talkin' bout? Bro, you don't just come out in the open talkin' like that unless you on some police shit. You didn't even tell me your name you just start talkin' bout some shit that I have no clue about!"

To make a long story short the guys name was Dirty Dee and he was legit. My only question was why would a dealer bring his customer around his source? That automatically cuts out the middleman! Plus, I was kind of disturbed because no one should have known what I was doing and where to find me. My intentions were to remain in the shadows and not to be a hands on guy. But after listening to Dirty Dee for more than 10 seconds I took a chance and exposed my hand to him.

Later on that day I received a phone call from a number that I didn't recognize. A woman with a smart mouth spoke through my earpiece and said, "Where your arrogant ass at? I'm bout to pull up on you right now."

I gave her my store location and this lady pulled up on me like she owned the place. I can't lie; I was amazed because I had finally met my match. LaRaye ended up being around me 24/7. She even made a list of demands about what I needed to do in order to upgrade myself for her. She said that my gold teeth had to go and that I was carrying around too much money on my person. She said it made me look like a dope boy and that was a turn off to a real woman. She also said I only had a certain amount of time to meet her demands.

Well, I also had some demands of my own. First of all, her long beautiful hair that I know she valued so much had to go. Secondly, her police boyfriend had to become a distant memory as of that day.

Now, I don't know who this dude was but she met my demands rather quickly. Within 24 hours she had changed her phone number, added me to her phone plan, and cut her hair as low as Halle Berry's on the movie "Boomerang." I was thinking that she was either crazy or she was really feeling my vibe.

LaRaye had even started taking trips with me out of town to take care of business. Everything was going well between Big Tee and I but his greed had become worse. He would get us all the way to Texas and then change the prices on us.

One time he had got us to Texas and told us that everything was all set up. But when the time to handle business came around, he completely stopped answering the phone. I was concerned because Big Tee was usually like clockwork. Something bad had to have happened because he knew that we had driven 9 hours with thousands of dollars in cash and to cut his phone off on us was not like him.

3 days went past with no word from Big Tee and my concern turned into anger. I had to think fast. I remembered that I had met Pimp and he was staying at the same hotel that we were in. Pimp had told me if I ever needed some weed he would call his dude for me.

I ended up catching up with Pimp and explaining my problem about how Big Tee had gotten us all the way to Texas and quit answering his phone. Pimp called his source and let him know that we needed some marijuana. Pimps source wanted $675.00 a pound and only wanted to serve us 10 pounds the first time to see how well business went. If everything went smoothly he would serve us more the next time.

I remember thinking "Hell Naw! I can't make no money with only 10 pounds at that price!" Plus I had too much money on me to drive all the way back to Memphis with and risk of getting pulled over by the K-9 team.

Pimp made a couple of calls to a few of his pimp partners and let them know that his peoples was in from out of town and was looking to make a move on some green. One of the dudes came through for us. Pops, an Old School Cat who he had been copping his smoke from. Now, the name Pops may sound like an old wrinkled dude, but "Naw." Pops was a city slicker and he didn't act like he was from Houston. He invited us out to his house and after I told him what I wanted he made a couple of phone calls and got me the 50 pounds I was originally trying to get from Big Tee.

We made it back Memphis safely and got rid of the pounds as quickly as usual. Even though I could afford to buy a hundred pounds I kept my purchases rather small. My profits were pretty good after paying all of my expenses from the trip.

Highway told me that he planned to bake a cake and get back at Big Tee in the near future now that we had found a new Source. Everything went well with Pops for a while. He did good business in the beginning but as they say all good things must come to an end.

The time came to serve Big Tee his dessert. We used a four man wrecking crew for this job. Highway, Highway's partner, Big Head Rick, and I brought along Bar Bar my counterfeit partner. I felt like this was a pretty sufficient crew but I was wrong.

Before we pulled-out to head to Houston to finesse Big Tee someone close to Highway had stopped by my store and told me that Highway and Big Head Rick had been making alternate plans without me. Their plan was for Big Head Rick, who would be driving the contraband car, to make a detour and take another route unbeknownst to me. First of all, I was stunned because this person knew about our business. Secondly, I was hurt because I looked at Highway as a big brother. I didn't want to believe it and until this day I can't prove the accusations to be true or false. But, I did put Bat Bar up on game because we were relatively close.

Highway and I placed the largest order that I had ever made at the time. I'm pretty sure that Big Tee knew that I had enough money to pay for the order a long time ago but I always kept my orders to a minimum. He obliged with my request and asked me if I was really sure that I wanted to get 75 pounds. He told me that by purchasing real large quantities my ticket prices would go down. But I didn't believe him because every time we got to Texas the prices would go up a little.

Once we arrived in Houston we camped out at a new location and told Big Tee that we'd handle the business there. I guess he felt bad about leaving us out there to dry the last time, so he didn't have a problem with the new location. He would bring us the 75 pounds to our new location and let us get the "Popcorn" for the same price we had been paying for the lower grade.

I had started to feel bad and wanted to back out at the last minute. I didn't feel comfortable because of what had been planted in the back of my head about Highway maybe trying to cross me out and ruin our friendship. But, the show had to go on.

The mission was successful, and everything went the way that we thought it would. But, all good things must come to an end. Not even 45 minutes outside of Houston, Big Head Rick got pulled over by the only State Trooper on the highway for the whole distance back to Memphis. Damn! Ain't life a bitch!

Big Head Rick was in the far right lane. Once he spotted the Highway patrolman sitting to the right he got over in the left lane but to make matters worse he forgot to turn on his signal light. Plus, we had called him ahead of time and warned him about the patrolman sitting there.

I guess it wasn't meant for me to ever find out the truth about the supposed re-route. Plus, we had actually lost a good plug. The more that I thought about it I began to realize that Big Tee was just trying to feed his family. There were times when he could have been foul and gotten me to Texas and finessed me out of my bread, but he didn't. But oh well. This drug game is a dirty game where you win some and you lose some.

After that botched, more of my luck just went down hill. Karma is a bitch! Pops started playing games. For a few trips he kept everything on the up and up. I had no reason to doubt his loyalty because he had actually brought us to his home where he laid his head.

We planned a trip to Texas to get about 50lbs. Pops had told us that the complete package was already at his house. His Sources had seen the way that we were doing business and so they just left the product there.

Well, once we arrived to Pops house we discovered that he only had 22lbs. He told us that his folks were going to bring the other 28lbs in the morning. Pops knew I was pissed so he tried to ease the tensions by serving me some lame ass game. He said he had some Mexicans on his team that would match me and front me a pound for every pound that I bought, and that the ticket would come down as our relationship grew.

I knew that it was a bunch of bologna as soon as the lie began to roll off of his tongue. It sounded good but why did I have to hear it from the middleman? The reality was that Pops had sold the 28lb right before we had arrived thinking that he could replace them before we made it to his house. But Pops little antics had ruined my plans. I had figured out a system for timing my departure and this unexpected delay had ruined it.

I had a decision to make. I could either leave with the 22lbs., or I could wait for Pops folks to bring the rest in the morning. Pops talked us into staying and even offered for us to stay at his house. We declined because I had brought LaRaye with me and Highway had brought his little cousin Joe Joe.

We got a couple of hotel rooms and the next morning turned into evening without the business being taken care of. And when we finally made the transaction I still ended up getting screwed. Pops took our money for the 28lbs. and went and bought some right compressed weed that smelled like mildew so that he could make a bigger profit.

I never thought to check the weed after we'd gotten it. Pops brought the weed and just threw it into the trunk with the rest of it. I didn't even notice it until we stopped for gas and LaRaye informed me that it smelled like something was dead in the trunk.

I opened the trunk and the smell almost killed me! I opened the luggage that held the marijuana that we had just gotten from Pops and up until this day that is still the worst batch of weed that I have ever seen! I called Pops but he just hit me with some lemon lame ass excuse. I went ahead and rolled with it but I knew that I had to get Pops a cake mix ready. His time was coming.

To make matters even worse, while Highway and I were playing lead car on the interstate we spotted a K-9 team as we were passing through East Baton Rouge, Louisiana. LaRaye and Joe Joe were tailing behind in the contraband car.

I saw it all happen in slow motion as the flashing lights got behind them and pulled them over. My heart dropped to my feet! I really didn't know what to do except to keep going. I remembered Joe Joe telling me a few days prior that if he ever got caught then he would take his own charge. All I could do was hope that he had meant what he told me.

A few hours later LaRaye's number showed up on my caller I.D. I didn't answer the first couple of times until she texted me and told me that it was actually her and Joe Joe had taken the charge. Joe Joe told the police that LaRaye was only giving him a ride and that she had no idea what was in the luggage. I was relieved to know that dude was solid.

I never did tell Pops about the loss. And we didn't return back to Texas for a while either. I just kept feeding

Pops excuses about how busy I was. But Highway and I did do a little business with him by putting enough money into his bank account to purchase five or 10lbs. until we could make up for the loss. He would mail us the contraband to various different addresses and he still had the nerves to play games by sending us bullshit. I guess he thought that we were country boys but I'm from a city where nobody is straight, and Pops would soon find out.

12

Same Guy, New Tricks

In the meantime Highway and I had started to find other ways to turn over an illegal profit. We hooked up with a dude named Peewee who told us that he had a pill plug in Los Angeles, California on 10 milligram Loretabs.

At first I was hesitant to do business with PeeWee because he was known for having fake everything from fake pounds of weed, to counterfeit money, and even fake bricks of cocaine. If you name it PeeWee had it but it wasn't real. So I really didn't believe that his connect was real, but I needed to make some bread fast. Our supply was drying up and our clientele was complaining about the trash that Pops was sending us.

We ended up going to California and just like Pee Wee had told us he really did have love there. It was like his second home! They totally loved him out there. He had at least three different plugs on marijuana, pills, and syrup. I couldn't figure out for the life of me why PeeWee rode around Memphis serving fake drugs when he could have the city sewed up with pharmaceuticals. I just didn't get it.

I placed an order for 10,000 Loretabs at $2.00 a piece and Pee Wee's people were there in less than an hour with the order. I was like damn! That's what I'm talking about! Getting straight down to business and not wasting time.

Even though the "Sunshine State" was a beautiful site

to see I wanted to hurry up and get back to Memphis to se how the pill selling process would work out. I remembered that my Aunt Tee had the same hustle but I have never witnessed her dealing so I was curious about how we would get our pills sold. The only thing I was sure about was that I would sell them one at a time.

The mission was simple: sell the pills as fast as possible and go back to California to get some more. We would take the mail route because there was no way that I was driving 23 hours across the country to buy some pills and drive them 23 hours back the other way. So, I learned to fly.

Highway was the man when it came to the road or the air. He would get to his destination. And to be honest, I actually loved flying. I was kind of used to it because I had to fly when I was in the Feds being shipped to different prisons. So flying wasn't new to me.

The hard part came when it was time to mail the package. The post offices in California were fully up on game about drug shipping, so we had to take extreme measures with the process. You could go inside a California post office with your package sealed tightly in order to avoid detection, make a payment for next day delivery and still not receive your package, That's because the clerks are trained to act normal, let you leave your package and then inform the Postal Inspector of the suspiciousness of your package being mailed overnight to one of their red flagged States that had been targeted as hubs for drugs being sent through the mail.

We decided that the risk was worth the reward. But, we would mail our packages from smaller counties outside of L.A.; we were always successful doing it that way.

Once we made it back to Memphis we found out that

our package had already made it there ahead of us. My next order of business was to learn this new process because I would be dealing with a new customer base and I didn't have any clientele for pills. Highway had to tell me what the pills sold for which was $4.00 a pill for a hundred pack and if you bought more we would drop the price down a quarter or fifty-cents.

When Pee Wee and Highway put the pills on the market they were gone faster than the first 20 pounds of marijuana that we sold. I couldn't believe that 10,000 pills had gone so fast! The drug game was the shit! I had doubled my money in no time.

The only problem that I had with the pill game was that Pee Wee wasn't consistent. He was taking a few other dudes on the same trip so we would have to wait too long to re-up. This caused Highway to come up with the idea of cutting out the middleman by getting the Connect's number himself.

In the meantime, Dirty Dee had started coming around more often and he told me that he had some Jamaicans in Houston that could get me some weed. I felt more comfortable with the weed even though the pills returned a better profit. It carried less jail time and a lower risk of losing the package.

The first time I tried Dirty Dee's folks in Texas they didn't keep it real. I dropped $2,500 into an account just to see if the guy would mail me 5lbs and he didn't come through. Dirty Dee knew how I felt about getting played for my bread so he made up for it big time. He said he had some guys out of Mississippi that was working with bricks of cocaine and he was willing to set up a deal and let me rob them and we'd split it 50/50.

I wasn't going to put myself in that situation at first because of the Karma that came my way after the Big Tee situation. The only person that I was willing to risk it all on was Pops for his treacherous deeds. But, the greedy part of me was like "Fuck it! Let's do it!" I told Dirty Dee that there would be a change of plans. If these dudes were really as sweet as he said then I would let my guys take care of the situation by making a fake purchase.

That move was a major success. Dirty Dee, Highway, Casper, Pee Wee, Big Nose, his little brother, Dinky, and I ate good off of that move. But I found out later that Dinky had tried to have all of us robbed. It's a dirty game but we reaped what we sowed.

We finally ended up getting the phone call from Pops that we had been waiting on. He said that he was in West Memphis, Arkansas, and he was heading back to Texas. I had come to find out that Pops took a trip to Kansas City, Kansas once a month. He had a cousin who played for the Kansas City, Chiefs that bought 200lbs every month like clockwork.

This time his cousin didn't want all of the pounds. I guess Pops must've tried the same greedy B.S. that he pulled on us, with his cousin and tried to hit him with a bad batch. Pops couldn't return to Houston with the marijuana because he had gotten it on consignment and returning to his Mexican plug without all of the pounds gone would show bad faith on his part. So he contacted us to see if we could take them off of his hands. He said that he would make sure that he straightened us out for the last bad batch that he served us.

I went to meet with Pops and told him to just leave the pounds with us and we'd have them sold by the time he made it back to Texas. I reminded him that I send my money to him up front all the time and now it was time for him to trust me. And let's just say that Pops never got paid and we never heard from him again.

Now I didn't have any way to get more marijuana. I was not going to pay $675.00 a pound from Pimps people and I couldn't go to Houston so soon knowing that I had people looking for me. So, I had to do the L.A. thing for a while.

I had decided to take things a little further with LaRaye. After dating her for a year, I moved in with her and her daughter. But I would still leave a few of my cars over my sister's house to make it seem like I was still living there.

One day I had gotten a call from my sister saying that her landlord had agreed to sell her the house that was living in instead of her continuously paying rent. So during the closing phase, some way or another my sister had found out that the house had about $30,000 worth of equity in it. The landlord and Real Estate Agent tried to somehow swindle her out of the money, so she needed me to come over and look over the deed to her house.

By the time I had gotten there my sister was standing in the front yard having a casual conversation with her landlord. But what struck me as rather odd was that the passenger in the landlord's car was staring me down. I could only tell that he had dreads and was wearing shades. I couldn't be too sure but it seemed as if he had a smirk on his face.

After the landlord and his strange passenger were gone, I asked my sister what was going on with the house situation. She told me that her Real Estate Agent was on some sheisty shit and was trying to steal the equity. Her landlord told her that he also noticed the Real Estate Agent was scheming but before he could give her the heads up she had jumped to conclusions. So the landlord wanted to talk to he privately but knew that she was angry so he brought his cousin with him for insurance in case things got out of hand.

My sister said that before she came outside to speak with her landlord she saw the dude that was in the car with dreads out of her front living room window walking around both of my Lexuses that I had sitting in her yard. I asked her if she recognized his face? She said she didn't and by the time that she walked out dude was already getting back in the car. I blew the incident off. I remember thinking that maybe the guy liked how I had the cars equipped.

A few days later I was at the barbershop and my cousin, Squirt, was in their getting his haircut as well. He told me that before I left he needed to holler at me about something, I was like bet.

So Squirt, his girlfriend, Mikey, and I went and sat in my LS 430, which was backed in in front of the barbershop. Squirt asked me if I minded if his girlfriend rolled a blunt in my car since he knew that I didn't smoke. Before I could say, "Yeah" out of nowhere a black Dodge Magnum comes and blocked me in.

The occupants of the black car were two Police Detectives. The driver had dreads and the passenger was bald headed. The driver flew to my side of the car, snatched me out and made me put my hands on the front hood. He immediately went through my pockets and asked me where the dope was.

Not knowing what was going on I asked the officer if he knew me from somewhere. He told me to shut the fuck up because he was the one asking all of the questions. He had his partner to keep an eye on me while he made everyone else get out of the car and searched them. The officer found some form of contraband on everybody except me. He even searched my car that came up empty also. So he pulled my cousin Squirt to the side and told him that if he would lie and say that he bought the contraband that was found on him from me, he would take me to jail, have my car towed, and he would let everyone else go free.

Come to find out, the Detective attended the same Church as Mikey and he sang in the Church choir. Nobody went along with the Detectives proposition and he let them all off with a warning. I don't think that my cousin would have told on me, even if he did purchase the contraband from me.

The Detective situation threw me for a loop. Why would be ask them to lie on me? I don't even know him! I hadn't had any encounters with the Cops and I was under the impression that my little drug business was running rather smoothly. But after that little situation all types of weird things started happening to me.

13

More Money, More Problems

One day after we opened up the store I pulled into the parking lot in my Corvette and parked in my usual spot. Big Nose was in the store stocking the beer cooler while Highway was behind the counter doing the same with the tobacco products. My cook Jeri was at the pizza station warming up the Hunts Brother's pizza machine, and my sister was at the cash register.

My vendors usually run in the a.m. and I had talked to one of them who worked for Mr. Pure's Juice Company and had been delivering me different flavored juices. He said that he was waiting for me at the store because I still owed him a check for a previous order over a week earlier.

Well, I hadn't been in the store for a whole 3 minutes yet, talking to the vendor about settling the debt when, in walks about 9 Memphis Police Department Organized Crime Unit Detectives telling everyone to freeze and not to move. Although they never showed me a search warrant they began searching my store immediately. They searched for about 45 minutes and came up empty.

One of the Detectives asked me whose revolver was sitting under the counter. While I was explaining to the Officer that I was the actual owner of the store gun I looked over to the side and had to do a double take. I saw one of the Detectives pull a clear bag with something in it out of his pocket and placed it in one of the cake boxes in the aisle where the cakes were kept.

After the detective looked through some more cake boxes he returned to the one where he had placed the plastic baggie and said, "Come here Lt. and look at what I just found!"

I said, "Ya'll can't be serious. I just saw you take that out of your pocket and put it there!"

I was told to shut up and the Lieutenant. called in the dog. Once the K-9 got there they spent another hour and a half searching the place. The detective who had the K-9, returned with some marijuana in a sandwich bag. They weighed it and discovered that it was a half an ounce.

I never sold anything under a pound so I had no clue where the half-ounce had come from. But I later found out that it was conveniently enough weed for the cops to charge me with a Felony. Supposedly the K-9 had detected the odor coming from a hidden area inside the wall in the back of the store. But after witnessing how the Detectives had planted the first evidence in the cake box, in order to have reasonable cause to bring in the K-9, I knew exactly where the baggie came from.

The Detectives tried to use the good cop, bad cop maneuver to corner us up. The good cop was a female Detective who pulled Highway and I to the side and said they had gotten a call that drugs were being sold out of the store and they wanted to know who it belonged to. Neither one of us claimed it.

Then the bad cop came along and said that we were all going to jail if no one took ownership of the contraband. Their technique wasn't going to work. None of us did anything.

The good Detective came back and said that we were being left off with a warning. She presented Highway and I with some type of paper to sign saying that the firearm they found under the cash register wasn't ours but that we had knowledge of the fact the gun was there. We basically laughed in her face. But after that encounter I had began to take the heat from the police a little more serious.

My sister had gotten a call from one of her Sources. The source had asked her about the meeting that she had had with her landlord. My sister confirmed the meeting and the presence of her landlord's cousin. Supposedly the cousin was brought along to be of assistance just in case my friends and I decided to start some shit about the plot to steal the check for the equity of the house.

I spoke with my sister's Source personally and was informed that the landlord's supposed cousin with the dreads was actually a Detective for the Memphis Police Department's Organized Crime Unit name Det. Therman Richardson and the guy couldn't stand me. I told the Source about my last 2 incidents involving Det. Richardson and the Source warned me to watch out for the guy because he hated those whom he believed were drug dealers. This guy was a stone cold hater! After finding out this information I didn't have any more problems with the Organized Crime Unit until years later.

Meanwhile, I had been talking to Pimp more frequently. I asked him to keep his eyes open in Houston for someone that I could score some weed from. I also told him about the business that I had been doing in California with the Loretabs. Pimp said that he could get me plenty of them but at a higher price, $2.75 a pill. I told him cool and that I would book a flight in a couple of weeks to come and check them out.

I was spooked from the last 2 police incidents and so I wanted to lay as low as possible. So in the meantime I wanted to get my credit score up into the 700's. So I began working on my credit score with J.T. A better credit rating would allow me to purchase things with no down payment and only a small interest rate.

So, in my off time from the drug game I started putting everything in my name in order to build credit; credit cards, furniture bills, cars, etc. I even went to Banks and took out small loans even though I didn't need them.

I was warned to be careful of credit-to-debit ratio. This when you have some credit to acquire things and you tell your lender that your yearly earnings are $80,000, for example. But when the lender pulls your credit they discover that your payout to other lenders is more yearly than what you reported. This will cause new lenders to be reluctant in their dealings with you. If they do decide to establish a banking relationship with you, they will seize the opportunity to charge you a very high interest rate on anything you apply for, such as cars, personal, or small business loans.

The way to remain in good standings with lenders is by paying your bills on time. If you have credit card bills, pay a little bit extra than what the monthly fee is but never pay the bill completely off. Just keep the credit card within the halfway point. Most lenders are greedy and by following the above advice most greedy lenders will turn a blind eye to your debt ratio. Trust me, I know. J.T. had all of this figured out and I got the opportunity to learn a lot of this information from him.

Now, even I know that nothing last forever. If I didn't plan my exit route soon the outcome would eventually lead to 2 things: either prison or jail. The signs were all there from the last 2 mishaps with the detectives. But my own selfish greed ended up getting the best of me in the end.

Highway, Big Nose, and I took a trip to Houston and hooked up with Pimp. Everything that he had told me on the phone panned out to be true. He got me served $3,000 tabs the first time and I even bought 5lbs of marijuana from his people for $675.00 a pound I ain't gone lie, when I first saw the weed it was like nothing I had ever seen before. I literally thought that somebody had taken off the head of the jolly green giant from the vegetable can. The smell was so loud that I as wondering how we would conceal it. Highway smiled and said that it would be easy if we just triple sealed it.

After we finished putting our package together Pimp asked us if his cousin could come up to our room. We agreed and Pimp introduced us to his little cousin named Pimp Jerry, who was also in Houston pimping. I asked Pimp Jerry why I hadn't saw him at the hotel before! He said that he lived in the 5th Ward with his females and every time he came I'd already be gone and headed back to Memphis.

Pimp and I exchanged numbers. He promised that he'd find me another weed connect. I was in need of a connect that wasn't afraid to sale over 5lbs to an out-of-towner on the first meeting.

Meanwhile, Pimp had made me a proposition that I couldn't refuse. He had offered to gather up as many pills as he could and purchase a few pound from his people and mail it all back to me in Memphis. He knew that this would save me some trips until I could find some cheaper prices. In return, he wanted to throw a couple thousand beans and a few pounds of his own in there for me to sell for him. His way we would both be doing one another a favor.

A deal was made that day and our operation continued for a while. We also continued to deal with Pee Wee whenever his California connection could provide us with 10,000 tabs. We'd fly out to Cali and take care of business.

I eventually grew tired of grabbing the small amounts from Houston because it had become too stressful. The profits weren't sufficiently covering my high spending habits and my bills were killing my pockets. Plus, Pimp had started wanting his money deposited in his bank account within no less than 2 hours after our package arrived. I was thinking 'Damn! He pimpin' for real!" So before I fell out with Pimp I just fell back from the Houston situation for a while.

One day this dude walked into my store to purchase a Black & Mild. After I rang up his purchase he pulled out a gold Rolex watch and asked me if I was interested in buying it. I grabbed the watch, put it to my ear, smiled and told him that it was a nice try. I then reached under the counter and pulled out the exact same watch except mine was silver. I told him that a lot of them had been floating around.

The guy introduced himself as Wild D and said the watch trick was just a play to get to talk to me. He said that he had just gotten out of the jail and the rumors were that I sold pills. He said that he used to sell pills also and he still knew plenty of people that wanted them. He also told me that he had an uncle out in Miami who was a player and a pimp whom he could hook me up with. I remembered Wild D right off the top of my head as the guy who had done an interview on the show "Gangland" when they done an episode about the L.M.G. projects in South Memphis.

In order for Wild D to convince me that his uncle was legit he placed a call in to him right there in my face. His uncle wanted to speak with me to confirm that he could get me what I needed and to make sure that I wasn't wasting his time. It was obvious that he had never heard of me before because if he had he wouldn't have questioned the way that I handle business.

As soon as I grabbed the phone the uncle asked me what my bankroll looked like. The question confused me, and he explained that it meant how much money did I have to spend. So I asked him what the ticket would be for 10-20 thousand beans. The uncle wasted no time telling me $3.00 a piece and that his price was non-negotiable. He gave me the options of either going to Miami to pick it up or calling his sister in East Memphis and dropping the money off to her. As soon as he got a confirmation from her then I would receive my package within 24 hours. I must admit that I was impressed by how fast these people were moving. It seemed as if they had already tagged me as a potential buyer.

I told the uncle that I didn't feel comfortable talking and negotiating when I didn't even know his name. He told me that his name was Dubb and that I should have his nephew Wild D show me who he was on YouTube. Dubb also told me that he was trying to sell a Ferrari if I was interested. He said that all of the vehicles that I would see on his YouTube channel were for sale and that he had two of each. Then the phone went dead.

I told Wild D that his uncle was too damn cocky. Wild D said that was just the way Dubb naturally was. I went ahead and sent some bread Dubb's way, maybe 2 or 3 times, and I always ended up being short a couple of hundred pills. So I told Wild D that I would stand down on that move because Dubb was already charging the shit out of me and I was spending too much money to turn over a profit. But Wild D and I remained in touch.

One day I decided to call Pimp Jerry to see what he had come up with. As soon as he heard my voice I could hear the excitement in his voice. He said he had lost his phone and my number and had been waiting on me to call. He said that he couldn't get my number from Pimp because they had fallen out over some stupid shit. Pimp Jerry proceeded to tell me that he had been dealing with a guy and he told the guy about me, and how nobody would serve me more than 5lbs of weed at a time. He asked me how much I was trying to buy? I told him that if it was what I liked and the ticket was proper, then, I wanted 50lbs.

Pimp Jerry said that he would find out if the 50lbs I wanted was available. He would even go and look at the weed to make sure it was worth purchasing and how much the ticket was. He called me back not even 2 hours later and said that the dude waned to talk to me personally. The dude got on the phone and told me that I would love the batch of weed he had, and it was the best on the North Side of town. He said that anybody could vouch for him, but I didn't need a witness I needed product.

So once again, Highway, Big Nose and I went to Houston. I can't lie, every time I returned to Houston I looked over my shoulders and was cautious about who I dealt with because of my past endeavors. When we arrived I called Pimp Jerry and asked him when he wanted to introduce me to his people. He said that he was instructed to bring us to the Source's house whenever we arrived.

I don't really remember the exact street the house was on but I do remember that it was in the 5th Ward. I really liked Pimp Jerry's style. He told me up front that he wasn't trying to make any money off of us. He said that if the meeting went well I could exchange numbers with the source myself and whenever I was in town he'd ride along with me to make sure that everything went smoothly. He assured me that his Source was good people.

Once we arrived at the dude's house we all did our formal introductions and he had told me that his name was Big Mike, And this dude was hug! He looked like he should have been a Defensive Lineman for an NFL team.

One thing that I learned about Texas was that there are a lot of middlemen. Big Mike took us to one of his people. Basically, the Mexicans have the entire product but they enlist a bunch of blacks who they assume they can trust to help them distribute the product to the black market. The middleman pays his price and then he adds a little something extra on it and everybody's happy.

When we got to Big Mike's people's house they brought me out 5 different strands of weed and they were all horse-hay! Plus, the prices on them were outrageous I was like, "Is this some type of joke!" I even considered that it may have been a staged Robbery.

I openly expressed how I felt. "I drove over 9 hours in possession of $35,000 in cash for this! But I can't do nothing with what ya'll just showed me." When Big Mike heard how much money I had brought with me he immediately started stuttering.

"Nah, baby boy. I got ya'll. I just gotta make a few more calls for you but I'm gone get you what you need," Big Mike said.

I guess he didn't want to lose out on his take of the money I had brought.

I talked it over with Highway and Big Nose who were both very uncomfortable just sitting around in the 5th Ward with that amount of cash on us, and so was I. But Pimp Jerry assured me that it was all love. So I decided to wait and see what he would come up with because I really needed a plug.

We hung out for what seemed like forever. A black Dodge Charger pulled up and out jumped this little short stocky guy with cornrows. Big Mike said this was the person we had been waiting on and that he was going to take care of us.

Once we got inside of the house, Big Mike and the dude went into another room. I guess they hadn't discussed prices over the phone and so Big Mike probably wanted to know how much the ticket was so that he could put his tax on it and make his cut.

They were gone for about 5 minutes and then came back in the room with maybe an ounce of weed. It was a little better than the garbage that I had just seen but I still couldn't do nothing with it no matter what the price was. I told the dude that I was from Memphis and that they were very picky about what they sold and smoked. Right then I saw a glow in the eyes of the guy with the cornrows.

The guy asked Big Mike why he hadn't told him that we were from Memphis. He said that had he known we were from Memphis he would have known exactly what to bring because he had some people form Memphis who he occasionally served through a different party. But the dude's next question was what let me know that we are living in a small world. He asked me if I had ever heard of his associate named Pimp? I asked him if Pimp stayed in the hotels off of Basinett whenever he was in town? He verified that was the same Pimp. I told him that I was the one who he had been serving his high priced ass weed to for $675.00 a pound. He looked at me for a second and then we both burst out laughing. I didn't know what was more funny, the way he had been socking it to my pockets or the fact that we were about to form an alliance and we both could feel it.

The dude introduced himself as Boogie. And let's just say that I ended up getting the 50lbs that I had came for and I loved the ticket price that I was paying for them. I did the business fairly that first time, in order to allow Big Mike to make his cut. But I didn't need a middle man pinching off of my bread so before I left I slid Boogie my number personally.

It amazed me how out of all the people that I needed the most I ran across the main one that had a plug on corn nuggets; that's what I called his weed. Plus, I didn't have to cut throat Pimp to get Boogie's number. But to be honest I didn't really want to meet someone whose weed was that high because no matter what I paid for it all I wanted was $900.00 a pound. My motto was that the faster that I dumped the weed off, the quicker I could make my profit, re-up, and then start the process all over again.

Highway made a couple more trips to Houston with me and went off to do his own thing. He went ahead with the California plug and eventually ended up catching a Federal bid. It killed me on the inside to know that the guy, who had made it all possible for me, was incarcerated. But I had to keep the business going as usual.

Big Nose and I had become inseparable. He was my right hand man and when you saw me, you would also see him. I fully taught him how everything went and how I wanted everything to go. In return, I allowed him to purchase his weed for the same price that I was paying. To be honest, I did the same thing with the majority of my associates, if I liked the person. If you fell into this category I would drop the price down to $675.00 a pound but in return for the favor you would have to get rid of my weed first. But, if you weren't one of the lucky people I wanted $900.00 a pound, no exceptions.

Big Nose called me one day and said he had some news that I wouldn't believe. I told him to try me. He told me that his children's mom had gone live on social media and said that he and I were homosexual. I told him that she was only behaving the way that scorned women behave. On top of that, was the fact that he was never at home and continuously used me as his alibi, when in reality he was out with all types of women.

Other people started running with the rumor and twisting it. It really got out of hand! I couldn't believe that after all of the years I spent having my way with the female species that God has placed on earth for all of mankind (and there are some beautiful women on earth) it boiled down to this. Like the saying goes, "more money, more problems."

14

Smooth Sailing...

I brushed off the rumors and got back to the money. Big Nose and I had been going to Houston maybe once a week, and sometimes twice. We officially started traveling by air. No more long drives for me, especially since Highway couldn't travel with us anymore.

Boogie would always have someone ready at the airport to pick us up. I preferred to use Bush International Airport instead of the Houston Hobby. Once we'd land our day was already planned. I would always have to get me a fifth of Hennessey, a Sonic Ice slushee, and a 2-liter Coca-Cola. Then we would hookup with Boogie at whatever location the weed was. I would get there and look over the weed and if I gave my approval we'd purchase it and never see the product again until we were back in Memphis.

The way that we made this process run so smoothly was by forming two different teams; Boogie's team in Texas and my team back home in Tennessee. What Boogie requested from his team was to take the weed to a remote location and to get it properly vacuum sealed. Then they would take the packages to different post offices throughout Houston in order to avoid arousing the suspicions of the postal employees by constantly going to the same post office mailing express packages to the same city. This is why we used a team because by Houston being so big and people coming into post offices everyday sending off packages, it would be hard to notice multiple people. Boogie's team members would also open up different Bank Accounts in Banks that were similar to the ones in Memphis. This way, when it was time for me to send him money in advance we could utilize this method and avoid the risk of losing the money in the airport with their strict security checks.

Big Nose assembled my team in Memphis and I enlisted as many people as I could to allow us to send packages to their address. In return we would give them anywhere between $200.00 and $500.00 dollars depending on who the person was. Sometimes we would take a quick risk and send the packages in our own names.

This process of me flying to Houston, looking at the product and then not having to touch it or see it again until I made it back to Memphis worked perfectly for a nice little minute. Boogie paid his team handsomely for their cooperation anything from $500.00 to $1,000.00 on every drop. They would get $500.00 if we just needed to use their bank account and $1,000.00 if we used their account and had them drop off a package. We had everybody flocking to us and trying to take the risk! It was mainly college students because Boogie kept his circle around him legit because he was a felon and had a pending Federal case for "Conspiracy to Possess 5 Kilograms of Cocaine." So he knew that one slip up would cost him his freedom.

Boogie also loved to party, so after our business was conducted, we would hit the malls and shop before we hit the Houston night scene. There was something to do every night in Houston. Some places always had a crowd and whenever we were in the city we were there.

We would always hit up "High Rollers" or "Dream" for the after party. These are two strip clubs in Houston that everybody attended. Especially "Dream!" That place has some of the most beautiful and thickest women that a guy could ever lay his eyes on. I mean real arm-pieces. I couldn't understand for the life of me why women who are so beautiful would display their naked bodies and be touched by strangers from all over the world just to make a dollar. But hey, I guess everyone has to have a will to survive.

I ended up making a trip to Houston to make Boogie a proposition that would make both of us a shit load of money. I had shown Boogie that I was about my business by how consistent it was and I wanted to form a partnership. I proposed to him that I would but anywhere from 50-100 pounds every week if I could get them for the same price that he was paying for them. I knew in the back of my head that Boogie would always make a small profit off of me but I needed the prices to go down some.

In return, I told Boogie that if he'd match the amount that I bought then I'd personally purchase all of his pounds at $750.00 a piece. It made perfect sense because I'd profit a quick $15,000 from Boogie's batch and still have my own to make twice as much off of. I even fattened up the deal by telling him that I'd even sell his package first and he'd have his money back in less than a week with a nice profit.

Not only did Boogie agree to the proposition but he wanted to take me to meet his plug, Karlos. He said that he and Karlos had been dealing with one another for years and Karlos knew how good of a businessman he was. He said Karlos might also be interested in expanding his empire by sending some of his product to Memphis on consignment. I told Boogie to just take me to him and let me do all of the talking. Like I said before, just give me some Hennessey and I'll take a live bear out of his skin.

When Karlos and I finally met the first thing he said

was that Boogie had told him a lot about me. My response was that anybody who has weed as good the weed that he had was a good friend of mine. We all shared a good laugh and then got right down to business. I made the same proposition to Karlos that I had made to Boogie only I didn't ask him to give me the pounds at the same price that he had paid; he would've laughed my ass right out of his warehouse. But I did offer him a sweet opportunity to make some money with me by fronting me 50-100lbs on consignment and I'd pay him $675.00 a piece for them. I explained to Karlos that my mission was to build a solid and trustworthy relationship and to make sure that everyone was happy in the process.

We made a deal that day and my weed operation evolved into a million dollar enterprise. Karlos kept me supplied with grade-A, top of the line, mid-level marijuana and my clientele in the Memphis area got larger. And the more wealth that I acquired the more I drank. I began to consume alcohol for breakfast, lunch, and dinner.

In May of 2010 LaRaye had called me and told me that she was pregnant. I took the phone off of my ear and looked at it as if she could really see me. I asked her about the device that she had gotten from her doctor, which was supposed to prevent pregnancy for up to 5 years. While she cried on the other end, LaRaye told me that the doctor said there was still a possibility that she could end up pregnant.

I went along with the flow and told LaRaye that I was happy. I told her that if God allowed me to get her pregnant despite the odds then it must have been meant to be. LaRaye gave me my first little princess and years later, after Acasia Watson was already in this world and had warmed up her daddy's heart, LaRaye admitted that she had her doctor to remove her Mirana device so that she could intentionally conceive a child by me. (Thank you LaRaye, from my heart).

I knew that with us bringing a child into this world, we would need more space than the 2-bedroom apartment we shared with LaRaye's oldest daughter. So I gave LaRaye permission to go out at my expense and to find a much larger place in a safe and secure environment. She made a great selection in an upper-class neighborhood. It was a 5-bedroom, 2-½ baths; 2-stall garage brick home in Cordova, TN. The house was valued at about $250,000.00. I felt like I was really moving up in life. I was financially straight, had provided my family with a dream house, and my street business was doing well at the time. But mama always told me, "Don't count all ya chickens before the last one hatch."

In the fall of 2010, my mother was living off of N. Watkins in the Frayser area. LaRaye and I had just pulled out of her driveway and not even 5 minutes later my phone rang. I answered it and the caller said, "Man, I'm glad you answered the phone, I didn't know if I should call or not, or if the police would answer your phone!" I told the caller to calm down and explain to me what he was talking about. The caller went on to tell me that the undercover police were deep in front of my mother's house and they had her sitting on her front porch,'

My heart started racing 100 miles an hour. I had just pulled away from my mother's house! What the hell was going on! I ended the call and explained to LaRaye what was going on. All I could do was wait and see what kind of charges would be brought up on my mom and to keep checking to see if their was a warrant out for my arrest.

Later on that night my phone rang and my mother's number popped up on the called I.D. I had consumed so much alcohol that it didn't event matter who was calling from mom's phone. Maybe it was her or maybe it was the cops calling me to tell me to surrender and turn myself in.

I answered and my mother said, "Boy, where you at?" Come pick me up, I'm standing outside of Channel 3 Drive off of Mississippi and Crump Blvd." I asked her where that was and she told me it was the Organized Crime Unit's headquarters. She urged me to hurry because she had a lot to tell me.

Once my mom got in my presence she filled me in on what was going on. She said that the Fugitive Task Force was called to her house because they were told that D'Angelo Bill, A.K.A Wild D was there and he was wanted for First-Degree Murder. Someone had tried to cash in on the reward by anonymously calling Crime Stoppers and offering a tip. Mom then told me they had located the 46 pounds that I had stored away at her house in the attic.

Now, although mom was taken to the O.C.U. Headquarters they couldn't charge her with anything because their search warrant didn't say anything about drugs and the fugitive wasn't found inside of her home. But that still didn't stop the O.C.U. Detectives from opening up a new investigation on me.

We had come to find out that Wild D was actually at my mom's house at one point-in-time. He called his child's mother and had her come over to pick up some money for his little girl. When she showed up she brought a car full of people with her and someone in the car spotted Wild D and made the call to Crime Stoppers.

Not only did I lose 46 pounds, but after that day my life would never be the same again. Mom said that the Detectives told her that they knew exactly who I was and that they didn't like me. They said they would make sure that either 2 things would happen to me; 1) they'd either break me financially, or 2) they'd intercept so many of my packages that the Mexican

Mafia would kill me. It seemed as if they had turned my weed selling into a personal vendetta.

I asked mom to describe the Detective who made the statement and to give me his name. But all mom could remember was that he favored Dogg the Bounty Hunter. I connected that description immediately to the Detective that was at "Bob's Market" when I caught them planting drugs in my cake box. My mother reported the incident to the internal affairs (big mistake).

15

Things Just Got Real

After the incident at my mom's house I switched up my routine. Instead of using residential addresses to receive my packages, Big Nose and I started using hotels. We recruited a new team of people and had them to rent hotels in their names. Once the room was secured they would let the clerk at the front desk know they had a package that would arrive the next day by mail, to go-ahead and sign for the package, and they'd pick it up before checkout time.

Boogie agreed with our new method. We told him that since the police had caught on to how we were sending packages to different residences in various locations then we'd just start receiving them through businesses. We would make them seem as if they were coming from other businesses and we wouldn't send any more large packages in order to avoid suspicion. Boogie informed his team in Houston about the new technique and we were back to business as usual.

On February 21, 2011 LaRaye and I introduced our daughter, Acasia K. Watson, into the world. I finally got to meet the little girl that kicked and gave her mother hell all night. The moment that I saw her, my heart just softened and I finally had the chance to see how it felt to have my own little princess. I gave my daughter a French name that I loved the meaning of; in fact, I had even purchased LaRaye a restaurant and named it after my daughter before she was even born.

I thought that the birth of our child would bring LaRaye and I closer, but it didn't. We began getting into more and more physical altercations because of my cheating and transferring S.T.D.'s to LaRaye. We both would find out when LaRaye would go to receive her monthly doctor's checkups. It became so common that she would go ahead and have her doctor prescribe me with some medication as well.

LaRaye was always threatening to leave me but she knew that I wasn't going for that at the time. So instead, she'd begun hitting me where it hurt the most, my pockets. At least once or twice a week I would have her to help me count up the proceeds from my illegal drug operations and afterwards, I would have her to stash my profits. I would keep the money out for my re-up and to pay off Boogie and Karlos what I owed them.

LaRaye knew that I trusted her so much that I would never question her integrity, or second-guess her judgment. Plus, she knew I was drunk most of the time and that I would periodically take money from my stash to buy things: a car, some furniture, a trip, etc. I had begun to recognize that the one thousand dollar stacks would always be a little short, anywhere from $40-$60.

When I asked LaRaye if she was counting the money correctly she looked at me and fed me a straight-faced lie. I had no real reason to doubt her because she could've gotten anything that I had, all she had to do was to let me know that she'd gotten it. I'll tell any man you can't beat a scorned woman at her own game.

Instead of me facing the fact that my ole' lady was stealing from me, I instead began to focus on my right hand man Big Nose. Even though he and I were still conducting business together at that time I just didn't trust him. I had no real reason why. I had gained a lot of love for the dude and his mom, so I knew that I needed a reason to cut him off completely, and that reason eventually came.

****

On November 2, 2011, Detective William Acred was conducting surveillance at 9133 Chastain Place in Cordova, Tennessee, which was the home of LaRaye and I at the time. He observed Mario McNeal, a.k.a Big Nose arrive in a 2004 Dodge Durango, which was the same vehicle that had been parked in front of his mother's home. Detective Acred watched as Big Nose removed a parcel from the vehicle.

Approximately 45 minutes later Big Nose and I exited the residence and I placed several large plastic bags in the trunk of a Chevrolet Impala that was parked at the residence. I also had two more vacuum-sealed bags full of marijuana that I placed inside the glove box. Then Big Nose and I began to leave.

Detective Acred followed us. He observed us make an illegal U-turn and pulled us over. Detective Gayler then utilized his certified drug-sniffing dog, Droupie, on the vehicle and the dog gave a positive indication of the presence of drugs. Big Nose and I were asked to step out of the car and Big Nose admitted that he had a bag of marijuana that fell out of his pant leg. The marijuana weighed 23.29 grams. The officers also located 7.2 pounds of marijuana in the trunk of the vehicle as well as 191 grams in two vacuum-sealed bags in the center console. The officers proceeded to get a search warrant for my house and they searched and recovered the following: 3.5 pounds of marijuana, 2 vacuum sealing machines, $63,741 in cash, and 2 handguns.

They took LaRaye, Big Nose, and I to the O.C.U. head

quarters for questioning. Big Nose and I refused to give any statements but it was passed on to me that LaRaye made a statement on me. I was blinded by love and I didn't want to believe that she would do such a thing. I never even asked my Attorney if she actually made a statement or not.

Big Nose and I were later taken over to the Memphis County Jail for booking and processing. Before we entered the sally port, Detective Acred asked me why I had sent my mother to the Internal Affair to make a false report on him. I denied having any knowledge of what he was talking about because he didn't have any resemblances to Dogg the Bounty Hunter. But Detective Acred gave me some food for thought when he told me to remember his badge number and his name.

After we had finished with the booking stage I asked Big Nose if it came down to it, would he take the charge for me and he told me flat out, "No" I was surprised to hear him say that but it didn't really phase me. I had been looking for a reason to fall back from Big Nose and he had just given me my reason.

I kept calling LaRaye until she finally picked up the phone. She told me that she had just gotten released and the Detectives kept trying to make her a statement against me. She said she refused and I have yet to see my tangible evidence to prove that she did. But, like I said earlier, I was told by another Source that she had indeed made a statement.

My bond was set at $65,000.00 and Big Nose's was set at $20,000.00. We both made our bonds and hurried to go and retrieve a package that was supposed to be arriving that day at the America's Best Value Inn hotel in West Memphis, Arkansas. We asked the clerk at the hotel if a package had come for Walter Mathis. She said that a package had come but she had her husband to store it until its owner arrived. She said that if we'd patiently wait in the lobby her husband would bring it along shortly. I asked her if she was the owner and she said yeah. Right then I knew that something wasn't right and I gave Big Nose the signal for us to get out of there quickly.

The owner had secretly pressed a silent panic button that automatically alerts the West Memphis Police Department. The alarm was probably installed in case of Robberies. By the time we reached our car there could've been 5 police cars heading in the direction of the hotel. But luckily, we were headed in the opposite direction getting on the interstate to Memphis.

After that close encounter I got a call from my sister saying that I had a warrant out for my arrest. When I asked her what for, she said that it was for "Manufacturing with Intent to Sell and Deliver. I had just made bond so I couldn't help but think that there had to be some sort of error in the system Downtown. I called my bondsman and asked him to look up the warrant and he verifies what my sister had already told me.

I went to the Sheriff's Office on or about November 9, 2011 and turned myself in to attempt to clear up the misunderstanding. But once I got there I found out the warrant was actually a new one. So once again, I was booked in and processed. I received the affidavit and it read as follows:

Detective William Acred obtained a search warrant for one of the cellular phones that Watson had in his possession at the time of the arrest on November 2, 2011. Your affiant observed numerous text messages to and from "Boogie" and bank account numbers where "Boogie" was telling

Watson to deposit money. Further   text messages from Watson to "Boogie" were providing addresses in Memphis, Tennessee, and West Memphis, Arkansas where packages should be   sent. These included one telling "Boogie" the address: America's Best Value Inn 2411 E. Service Rd, West Memphis, Arkansas in the name of W. Mathis. Also that next day your affiant observed jail tapes from S.C.S.O officer Dunn for Kendrick Watson. On November 3, 2011 at 11:07 hours, Watson placed a phone call to LaRaye Harris, who was no longer in custody, asking her to go to American's Best Value Inn in West Memphis and get an express mail package in the name of Walter Mathis. Detective Acred then went to the location and met   with a Memphis Drug Task Officer and recovered a package in the name Mr. W. Mathis that had been delivered to the hotel. A search warrant for the package was obtained and it was found to contain 16.0 pounds of marijuana.

After I read the "Affidavit of Complaint," I knew why the front desk clerk had tried to get me to wait in the lobby. The police had already informed her that if someone came by looking for the package that she should call them immediately. So her intentions were to have me wait around while she called the police to come and apprehend me.

While reading the affidavit I noticed subtle hints of underhandedness used in order to catch me up. It was evident that they were going through my phones before they obtained a Search Warrant. Then once they stumbled across something they could use in court, they went and got a Court Ordered Search Warrant.

I knew that I could deal wit the legal details of my case later. My immediate concern was getting my bond set so that I could get out before all of my other cases popped up in the system. I was already out on a $25,000 bond for a pill case that I had caught in 2009 with my road dog, Yo-D, and that case was still pending in Criminal Court. This made it very likely that if I was still in jail by the time that the Prosecutor found out I had caught 2 new cases, he would recommend that all of my bonds were revoked pending the outcome of my original case.

They took away my clothes and gave me some standard issued jail clothes to put on. I was pissed off because LaRaye hadn't came and posted my bond yet. I mean, how much could a bond actually be for 16lbs of weed?

The next morning I was summoned to go to Video Arraignment Court. This is a process where you go before a Judge on a TV monitor and the Judge tells you what you are being charged with and how much your bond will be. When I finally got in front of the monitor I didn't hear anything that the Judge had to say except that my bond was being set at $350,00 for 16bs of marijuana. It was completely ridiculous! I was being treated as if I had killed someone!

I talked to LaRaye later on that day and she told me that no bail bonding company wanted to touch the bond because it was so high, on top of the fact I was already out on 2 separate active bonds that would eventually be revoked.

A couple of weeks later I was placed on the third floor, 3A. My cellmate's name was Ryan Vaughness, a.k.a Jack Frost. He and I used to kick-it in the cell like long lost relatives. He told me that he was charged with a home invasion, was on Federal probation, and that his first offer was 25 years at 100%, meaning that they wanted him to do the time day-for-day.

Jack Frost asked me if I knew a guy named Big Head, from South Memphis. I told him yeah, that I was familiar with him from being cell mates when I as in the Federal Penitentiary. He then asked me that if I bonded out would I do a him favor. He wanted me to help him contact his victims to see if they would drop the charges against him. I told him that he had my word that once I was released I would contact Big Head to see what I could do.

I felt like I could get somewhere with Jack Frost. I told him about all of the Detectives that I as having problems with: Det. Therman Richardson, Det. William Acred, and Det. Johnathan Overly, who was Acred's partner. I explained to him about how the Detectives were starting to scare me and how Det. Richardson personally told a Source he didn't like me.

Jack Frost and I remained cellmates until I bonded out on December 27, 2011. I gave him some numbers to keep in contact with me and gave him my word that I would do the best that I could to help him make light of his situation by connecting him with Big Head. Then I made my exit from the Jail.

LaRaye and Acasia were waiting for me outside of the Jail at 201 Poplar. They were sitting inside of my mom's Jeep Liberty that I had bought for her because the O.C.U. had seized all of our other cars. They claimed that they were under Investigation Hold, but in all actuality it is just a phrase that is used by the police to get more money out of alleged drug offenders. They take the cars and give you the option to buy them back at the book value, a process that would take up to a year. The process worked because most people don't want to just lose their vehicles especially if they have a lot of money invested into them. No one wants to see someone else riding around the city in his or her hard earned vehicles.

But for now our cars would have to stay put. I had to

figure our some other things like finding a new place to live. There was no way that we could possibly keep the house in Cordova, TN after the police had totally wrecked the place. Plus detectives Richardson and Overly had gone to my leasing managers at the restaurant that I had purchased for LaRaye and told them that I was a drug dealer. And so I had to break that lease also.

Detective Acred had also contacted the I.R.S. and had gotten a freeze placed on our tax refund for the restaurant, even though the refund had already been audited and cleared. The F.B.I. investigated the refund and all of the information that I had provided to get the refund, and could find nothing illegal. But, to this very day we have yet to receive our refund in the amount of $20,000.

LaRaye had a business account with the Bank of America that she had placed my name on just in case something happened to her then I would have access to that account. Well, Det. Acred had a freeze placed on that account too. He never showed any proof of drug proceeds being placed into that account, so I hired a Civil Attorney to fight it.

I knew the fight to unfreeze our funds would be a long drawn out process so I had to figure out another strategy to get paid. I needed to take a trip but I wanted to lay-low for a couple of months to let things die down. In the meantime LaRaye landed a job working at a Call Center selling Insurance. She knew that she couldn't go back to work at her father's restaurant as long as she was with me. Her father had heard about some of our physical altercations and he really disliked me, which I totally understand. *(I want to take a moment to say that if this book ever comes across your hands that I apologize to you as LaRaye's father, from the bottom of my heart. No man should ever put his hands on a woman.)* I didn't want LaRaye working for anybody else because I wanted her to be available to my every beckoning call.

I went into seclusion and tried to drink all of my sorrows away. I would go over to my mom's house everyday feeling sorry for myself because I had taken a fall when I was used to always being on top of my game. There was a young guy named Flopp who would come around quite often. When I was at my mom's house I would either go to North Memphis to pick Flopp up or he would come to meet me. I had been keeping him updated about the latest turn of events involving my legal woes and how I didn't know if I wanted to continue hustling because I had 2 pending drug cases. I didn't want to catch another one because the Judge would revoke my bonds for sure. I told Flopp that I was contemplating just taking my family and leaving Memphis, and Flopp agreed.

One day while Flopp and I was sitting out in my mom's yard just chilling, this guy named Lil' Rin, pulled up. He got out of his car and said that he had been trying to catch up with me. He said he'd seen me outside my mom's house one day but by the time he'd made his runs and came back around, I was already gone. He mentioned guys had been gossiping in the streets about my financial status, saying I was broke and couldn't make my bond. He went on to say that every since he'd known me, he'd always seen me on top and that the streets needed good dudes like me. He encouraged me not to let them see me sweat. Lil' Rin was later killed in a police altercation (R.I.P.). But I took everything that he said into consideration.

But the straw that broke the camel's back was when I called LaRaye at work one day and she didn't answer the phone. I was pissed off! She finally called me back and said that she wasn't able to answer at the time because her boss was around. I told LaRaye that she was her own boss and I made her quit that job that day.

I had LaRaye and my mom to start looking for a new commercial building so that I could buy them a new restaurant. And that's exactly what I did. We called the restaurant Soul*lucion Fish and Wing Palace. We opened up one on Lamar Ave. in Orange Mound and another one right across the street from the 201 Poplar County Jail. If the detectives wanted to harass me and stalk me so badly then they wouldn't have to drive far. They could just walk right across the street and take all of the pictures they'd like. But they could also use their 10% discount that we offered to Government Officials and dine with us. Once they were done eating they could walk back across the street and continue taking pictures.

I called Boogie and told him that I needed to make a trip. Since the mailing system was hot I had found another way that we could traffic our contraband from Texas to Tennessee. I let him know that I would be flying out there and I wanted him to meet my man Flopp. I knew that I had to be careful because Det. Acred had already shown me that he was a formidable adversary.

Flopp and I made our first flight to Houston in the Spring of 2012. Once we landed, Boogie's people picked us up. I wanted Boogie to get a good read of Flopp and the two hit if off instantly. Once I told Boogie about my new plan of moving our contraband through the Mega Bus he was on-board. Mega Bus was a new company and a competitor to Greyhound. They were trying to become a force in the transportation market and needed as many customers as possible, as they didn't have a luggage checking system. I figured if this idea failed, we'd just go back to our old routes: Car tailing and mailing.

I told Boogie to give me about a week so I could gather up some more participants. I also had to figure out a way to keep my people from seeing Boogie's face. The plan was for Bogie to prepare the package and to have his people hand it off to my people at the bus terminal when they got off of the bus. Then, once everything started flowing smoothly I would allow Flopp to handle all of my business for me so that Boogie could either call him directly or have his people call him. I needed to stay as invisible as possible because the Narcotic Agents were aiming at my neck.

16

New Businesses, New Allies... Same Problems

I started putting more time into my restaurants and I also started up my own record label called Money Train Music Group. My office and studio was downtown on Union Avenue. I signed a Memphis female rapper named Lil' Chat, formerly of the group Three 6 Mafia; Mac E; and a group called Hard Squad. Lil' Chat and I would do open mic nights on Wednesdays at my restaurant on Lamar Ave. We wanted to give all of the local artists the opportunity to showcase their talent in front of a crowd.

One Wednesday Lil' Chat and I held a Talent Showcase where we had 25 different acts from rap, to R&B, and spoken word, to stand-up comedy. The winner would take home $5,000.00 in cash and prizes. At the end of the competition a comedian by the name of Mouth Peace won. This dude was a natural and he was very talented. I brought him back a couple nights after that to do his own show and I allowed him to bring his own roster of up-and-coming Comedians from throughout Memphis.

Mouth Peace and I got along just fine because I was a big fan of stand-up comedy. Our conversations eventually shifted to the drug game. I guess Mouth Peace assumed that I was dealing in illegal contraband because of the way I was living. While I was always throwing money around without trying to turn over a profit, Mouth Peace said he was working for Memphis Light, Gas, and Water (MLGW), and after he'd finished paying his and child support he'd be broke with hardly enough money left to live on. I told him that I would consider helping him to find something he could make more money from. I also told him that I wasn't quite sure he was ready for the kind of lifestyle I was living.

I kept my eye on Mouth Peace for a few more months. He would throw a card game at his house every Wednesday from 7 p.m. to 12 a.m. He'd invite a lot of his coworkers and they'd just hangout. I knew that I needed a new storage spot to keep my weed, some place that would be least expected, right in the hood, and Mouth Peace's house was just the spot. I just had to figure out how to make it work.

So, I ended up letting Mouth Peace transfer his card night over to Soul*Lucion and blend in some comedy on a permanent basis. In return, he'd let me use his house to store my contraband and I'd give him $1,600.00 a month, not including what I'd give him if he decided to make some runs to Houston for me. Either to drop off money or pick up contraband and bring it back on the Mega Bus.

I kept my word to my old cellmate Jack Frost by getting in touch with Big Head and letting them air out their situation. I even helped him advance his financial situation. He'd send his wife to come and pick up money from me on a consistent basis. I told Jack Frost that I didn't want to deal with anyone new so only his wife could come to me. I wanted her to deal directly with me because I would've felt really bad if I'd sent her to one of my guys and something went terribly wrong. So his wife even came a few times to get contraband from me to serve to his cousins. What I didn't know was that Jack Frost had his wife to sign on as a confidential source with the Organized Crime Unit Detectives William Acred, and Johnathan Overly, who were the exact same agents I told him about when we were cellmates. I would find all of this out on a later indictment.

I eventually pled guilty to three years of Probation for the weed that was found at my house during Big Nose's and my arrest. I also pled out to an additional three years of Probation for the marijuana that was sent to the hotel in West Memphis, Arkansas. I was pissed! I kept asking my lawyer why'd the Prosecutors want me to take 6 years of probation for that small amount of weed? He told me that if I didn't take the offer the Prosecutor, Paul Hagerman, was offering me that he'd send the two weapons they found over to the Feds and things would be a whole lot worse.

After I took the deals, I went back to hustling full-time. I started dibbling-and-dabbling in the cocaine market. I'd buy a half of a kilo from Boogie and he'd front me another half of a key. I'd make a $15,000.00 profit in one day and I'd do it maybe three times a week.

Things went well for me for close to 2 years. I was bringing in a lot of money and in return I'd pay my respect to the streets of Memphis by hosting community events; Christmas give-a-ways, Mother's day barbeques; and 3-on-3 basketball tournaments to try to bring a little peace to a city that's divided by so much violence.

On Halloween of 2013, Boogie and I had begun to air out our differences and we threw our 3rd Annual Halloween Party. This event was probably one of the best days of my life. Boogie and his crew drove in from Houston for the event, and my man's 38 and Zack Randolph stopped through, also. There was a dance contest for the sexiest lady with the best costume. I was so wasted that I gave away about $3,000.00 to the winner. That young lady went home very happy that night!

Even LaRaye and I actually got along for the occasion. We ended the night by going to the Gentlemen's Club called, Pure Passion. I had so much fun during our Halloween extravaganza that I told Big Nose to plan us a Christmas party.

It was supposed to be cold during that time of year in Memphis but we were still getting 75-80 degree weather. I had just bought the new 2014 Sting Raye Corvette. The car wasn't even due to hit the streets until 2014 but if you knew the right people you could pay an extra $15,000.00 and they'd make it available to you immediately and build it to your satisfaction.

The decision to purchase the car came about because of a phone call that I had got one day from my guy Boo Dirty. He said that he'd heard that my money was funny and that I didn't have more money than my other guy Black Haven. People were saying that Black Haven was the one with all the money and cars. I took the phone off of my ear, looked at it and asked Boo Dirty if he really knew who I was. I told him to tell Black Haven that I was going to get a car built in his name and it would be all black. And that's how I ended up with the Sting Raye.

I told Big Nose that on our Christmas Party fliers we needed to tell all of the ballers to bring their whips out. By that time I had my XJL Jaguar on 26-inch rims in the paint shop, my S 550 Mercedes with 24-inch rims and a new paint job, my Porsche truck, my Hummer, and my other fleet of luxury cars that I had all ready and prepped for the event. But it never took place.

On December 13, 2013, LaRaye called me after she had left her Civil Hearing. The one she had against the Memphis Police Department's Organized Crime Unit for freezing her

Bank of America account, during our arrest in 2011. She said there was an African American Detective with long locks in his hair that showed up talking greasy to her because she was suing the Memphis Police Department. He told her to tell me that my days were numbered in the streets. Our conversation ended with LaRaye telling me not to panic. I eventually told LaRaye that I was familiar with the Detective and that his name was Therman Richardson. I gave her the history on him and I and told her I thought he was crooked.

On December 15, 2013, I was at the Gentleman's Club with a couple of guys when out of nowhere a short stocky dude walks up to me and say, "What's up Mr. Soul*Lucion." I just stared at him because the situation was kind of awkward. I told my guys that something wasn't right because I'd never seen the dude before in my life. I left the club that night spooked because I didn't know if the guy had been sent by Robbers to positively identify me. I later found out that Det. Richardson had sent him in there to keep an eye on me and to get updates about my movements in the Club.

The next day on December 16, 2013 LaRaye, my daughter, and I were awakened by some loud noise outside our door. I got up to look outside of the window and our home was surrounded by a S.W.A.T. Team of Police Officers. LaRaye and I slipped on our housecoats and opened up the door. We were lead outside in handcuffs while the lead Detective told us that his name was Sargent Ross from Desoto County Sheriff's Department. He said that the noise we'd heard were Blue Flashers that they shot out in order to wake us up and that the only reason they didn't kick in the door was because we had a baby in the house.

They placed both LaRaye and I into the back of a S.W.A.T. truck and told us that we'd be able to go back inside of our house shortly. Maybe 15 minutes later the back door of the truck was opened and staring me in the face was no other than, Det. Acred. LaRaye and I just looked at each other at the same time.

We were lead back into the house and reunited with our daughter at the kitchen table Sgt. Ross showed us an "Affidavit of Complaint/Warrant" and said that I wasn't under arrest but my house was. They were there to search my house and if they found anything illegal then I'd be charged with it. He also said they were there to confiscate all of my cars, jewelry T.V.'s, etc.

Sgt. Ross eventually took LaRaye out of the kitchen and told her that he knew she was a licensed gun carrier and asked her where she kept her weapon. She lead him into the master bedroom's bathroom closet where she kept all of her belongings and gave him two hand guns and an undisclosed amount of cash. The cash and guns were in a single suitcase. The rest of the house was searched and they discovered some more cash in one of our upstairs couches, but they found nothing else.

LaRaye noticed that one of the F.B.I. Agent's on it. She immediately said she didn't believe the man was an F.B.I. Agent. I didn't believe so either because they would've been the ones controlling the scene instead of assisting, but that was only our belief.

After not discovering any contraband Det. Acred and Sgt. Ross walks in the kitchen and tells me that I am under arrest for the two fire arms because they weren't properly stored inside a lock box and LaRaye didn't have them on her person. I was cuffed, lead out of the house, and taken to Hernando, Mississippi to be booked and processed.

Later on that night I was given an extremely high

bond of $100,000.00. I figured they'd set the bond that high because they didn't think that I could make it, but I did. I bonded out and when LaRaye picked me up that night she explained to me that Flopp, Mouth Peace, and 2 other guys from Houston were also arrested.

Apparently, while I was being detained they confiscated 54 pounds of weed, some guns, and other contraband from Mouth Peace's house in North Memphis. The Detectives had tailed Flopp and his girlfriend to the bus station that morning where they had picked up two individuals and drove them back to Mouth Peace's house to put away the luggage. Then all 4 went downtown to eat breakfast at my restaurant, where they were detained, minus Flopp's girlfriend. But for some strange reason they'd all been released without being charged.

The whole ordeal had me in panic mode. I felt like something wasn't right. I mean, how could they just walk away with no charges? I started thinking that maybe the guy at my house actually was F.B.I. and they were about to do a big sweep.

The next day I contacted my Probation Officer to report the incident and she told me to come into the office. Once I showed up she explained to me how the Prosecutor, Paul Hagerman, had called her and requested that she violated me immediately. I remember asking her why a Prosecutor would call her directly. She said that she had no idea but that she wouldn't submit my violation until after the holidays.

After the New Year, I went out and bought LaRaye and I two new vehicles until I could find out exactly what was going to happen to me. One day, I was pumping gas at the station on Polar when this dude named Lando walked up to me out of nowhere. He said he had just gotten out of jail and that the police had taken everything from him. I was thinking about how Karma is a bitch because I had just asked Lando to loan me some money because I was afraid to go to my stash and he quit answering his phone.

Lando asked me to give him a ride home. I agreed and along the way he told me about how he had just purchased about 40lbs of weed from another supplier and the next thing he knew his door was being kicked-in by the police. He said that the detectives asked him about me and told him that he might be getting indicted with me on some more charges at a later date. I found out later that Lando made a major statement against me and after reading it I could tell that he'd known he was breaking the code of the streets because he stopped the interview right in the middle of it.

17

The Sh*t Hits the Fan

On or about February 21, 2014, two Homicide Detectives walked into my restaurant. I knew they were from the Homicide Division because I remembered their faces from the hit T.V. series, "The First 48". The two detectives walked up to the cash register and told LaRaye to come with them and then placed handcuffs on her right in front of customers during lunch hour.

A few hours had passed before LaRaye returned. She said once she was inside of the Detectives vehicle, one of them told her that she wasn't really in any kind of trouble. They had to make it seem real in front of me. They took her to the Homicide Office and placed her in an interview room, and minutes later Det. Acred walked in.

Detective Acred asked LaRaye if she wanted to make a statement against me. When LaRaye refused Det. Acred reached into his folder and presented her with a bunch of text messages from my phone to and from other females and also pictures of different women and me together in different places. I could see it in her face that she was devastated but she continued telling me what happened. After she still refused to cooperate with the Detective, he told her to walk back to the restaurant in the freezing cold. I went to the Internal Affairs and made a report for harassing her. The Memphis Police Department's Office of Internal Affairs in the year 2014 was the worst group of Detectives that the citizens of Memphis could've had.

Then Déjà vu hit me again. On the morning of February 24, 2014 myself and 18 other defendants (6 from Houston) were all indicted by the State of Tennessee. That morning LaRaye had gotten up before me because she had to go back to the Internal Affairs to get a copy of her complaint, then she had to go, and open up the downtown restaurant. When she left the house she noticed a black pickup truck sitting down the street from our home and if pulled off right behind her as she left out of our sub division. She somehow got the license plate number of the truck and called me with the details and texted me a picture of the truck that was following her. I was confused because if it were, in fact, the Police with a warrant for my arrest why wouldn't they just utilize the Desoto County Sheriff's Department since they were supposedly working as a Joint Task-Force.

I jumped up and began drinking some Absolut, as I got dressed. I had a 10:30 a.m. meeting with the U.S. Representative, Steven Cohen. I wanted to speak to him about the behaviors of the City's Officers and to see if he could lead me in the right direction. When I left the house I didn't notice anyone following me but as I crossed over the State lines into Tennessee, I was immediately pulled over not even 15 feet from the State sign by an unmarked Dodge Charger.

I was removed from my vehicle and placed under arrest for warrants out of Memphis. Right before I was placed into the police car, the exact same black pickup truck that had followed LaRaye pulled up with the passenger window rolled down. Staring me in the face from inside the truck, with a smirk on his face, was none other than Det. Richardson. He stared at me for like 5 seconds, rolled his window back up and then pulled off.

I was then transported to Tillman Precinct in

Binghamton, North Memphis, where I was placed into a large white U.P.S. type truck that read "Memphis Police Department" on the side. The truck was equipped with 10-12 small standing only cages. About 10 minutes later, one of my closest friends was also detained and placed inside of the truck.

Before we were escorted downtown one of the Detectives received a phone call. On the other end was Det. Acred instructing the Detective to inform me of all the offenses that I was being charged with: Especially Aggravated Robbery; Especially Aggravated Kidnapping; Convicted Felon in Possession of a Firearm; Conspiracy to Commit UPCS with intent to sell more than 300lbs of Marijuana; Conspiracy to Commit UPCS with intent to sell more than 300 grams of Cocaine; and Money Laundering.

After the Detective read me all of the offenses, instead of having a heart attack, I just smiled and told Det. Acred that he's thrown everything at me except the kitchen sink. I know that the charges were a bunch of trumped up bull crap. I hadn't robbed or kidnapped anyone!

Normally booking and processing takes all day at the 201 Poplar Jail but for some reason our bonds were already set. Mine was set at a million plus, and the rest of my Co-defendants bonds were no less than half a million. Ugh Moe found out that he was being charged with all of the same violent offenses as me. But he and I had never committed such violent acts together. Also during booking and processing I saw Mouth Peace, Flopp, my cousin Marlo, and a few other associates.

We were all separated, and I was placed on the 4th floor in K-Pod. I would remain there for the next 23 months. Once I got myself settled into the pod, I placed a call in to my sister because LaRaye wasn't answering her phone. My sister explained to me that LaRaye had been rounded up during the sweep, along with my female friend Big Baby and Ugh Moe's girlfriend Skinny. All of their bonds had been set at $150,000.00.

The following week we all had Court. While I was sitting in the holding tank waiting to be escorted into the courtroom, all of my co-dependents (minus the 3 females, and the 6 people from Houston) were piled into the holding tank with me. Once we began talking, we realized that neither of us knew how the dots were connecting us together.

I remember Ugh Moe telling Flopp that something wasn't right about him. He said that every since Flopp's 2013 arrest he had been very distant. Marlo pitched in and told Flopp that if he found out that he's snitched then there was going to be some problems. Flopp tried to explain that he'd never snitch and that everyone had it all wrong.

During the melee in the holding tank, I noticed Mouth Peace was absent. I know for a fact that he'd been booked and processed right along with the rest of us on the day of our arrest. But foul play never dawned on me because I was too busy pondering that I might be sitting next to a real like snitch named Flopp.

A short time later all of our names were called by the Sheriff's Deputy, we were told that we'd all be going to Criminal Court Division 7 in front of the Honorable Judge Lee V. Coffee. I had heard so many horrible stories about this African American Judge! He used to be a Prosecutor and when he took the bench he still approached every case as if he was prosecuting the accused. Flopp's name was called and he walked out of the holding tank with the rest of us but before we got on the elevator to go up to the Courtroom he pulled the deputy aside and whispered something to him. After that I didn't see Flopp again for 3 ½ years.

My name was called. I entered the courtroom and stood in front of Judge Coffee for the first time with sweaty palms. I was shaking in my boots because I was thinking that with so many serious charges in a Courtroom as strict as Judge Coffee's there was a good possibility that I'd never see the free world again.

I looked over at the Prosecution table and saw the Assistant District Attorney, Paul Hagerman, reading off my charges. He went on to say that I had been the subject of a wiretap order that was issued out of Criminal Court Division 6 by the Honorable Judge John Campbell. On November 15, 2013, Detective Johnathan Overly from the Organized Crime Unit submitted an application/affidavit asking for my cellphone to be intercepted for the period of 30 days.

At that moment everything started to make sense. But I just stood there and listened while the Prosecutor alleged that I had committed all of these acts in just 30 days, which lead up to my phone being tapped. When he was finished, the Judge asked me if I could afford on Attorney. I told him "Yes" and he set me a new court date about 30 days away.

Once I got back to my pod I got on the phone to make sure that LaRaye was going to be able to make her bond. I couldn't stomach the fact she and I were both in jail while our daughter, Acasia, was out there by herself. My sister told me that she had in fact talked to LaRaye and she was pissed off at me. Apparently, they had placed LaRaye and my female friend Big Baby in the same housing pod and Big Baby told LaRaye that I'd denied our child. Eventually the women made bond.

I hired my first lawyer Robert Parish. He came to the Jail to visit me and after we'd made our introductions he told me that he'd worked well with the Prosecutor over my case. He told me that he personally had Judge Coffee's phone number but that it wouldn't help me any. I remember wondering why in the hell would he tell me some useless ass information? He also told me that he'd already heard about me before because my name had been ringing in the Prosecution's Office, which was a place where I wasn't well liked. The attorney also told me that a few of his clients were trying to offer some information against me in order to get relief on their own sentences.

I just allowed the Attorney to talk while I observed his demeanor. A red flag for me was when the clown had told me he was one of the "Top-Ten Best Defense Attorneys" in Memphis. I knew this was a false statement because I'd never heard of him. Unless lawyers were winning big trial cases in in Criminal Court they wouldn't have been highly recommended.

I asked "Mr. Top Ten" to find out what the offer from the Courts would be. He said he'd find out after he'd gotten the Motion-of-Discovery, because he'd spoken to Mr. Hagerman before coming to see me and found out that it was over 1,500 pages and discs of conversation. We shook one another's hand and he left.

My sister came to see me and I told her everything that my attorney said. I told her that I felt like it was a conflict of interest for my lawyer to have represented clients in the past who wanted to rat me out. But there I was being represented by "Mr. Top Ten," himself.

Eventually rumors had began floating around the Jail that I was snitching. My co-defendants had started saying that I must've somehow gotten caught up before our indictment and then started setting-up everybody else. Now this was just a theory because no one had yet seen the Motion-of-Discovery due to the fact the State hadn't finished preparing it. The rumors had me steaming hot because I despise slandering. And in Memphis there are a lot of envious people who'll get a hold of a false rumor and start beauty shop gossiping. That's just how it goes in Memphis.

I had grown impatient with my Attorney because a few weeks had passed with no sign of him. He showed up early on my second court date and informed me that he had only received bits and pieces of the Discovery packet, therefore he hadn't had enough time to look it over, so my case had to be reset for another 30 days. My Attorney would make a second visit to Jail to allow me to review the Discovery.

I knew that with the kind of charges I had, I was looking at a lot of time. But what was really puzzling me was why our case hadn't received any kind of media attention. I wasn't even in the Commercial Appeal Newspaper.

"Mr. Top Ten" eventually came over to the Jailhouse and went over certain parts of the Discovery with me. He gave me his opinion and it wasn't anywhere close to what I wanted to hear. He said that in all of his years of practicing law he's never seen an "Affidavit of Complaint" as well prepared as the one done in my case. He believed the State had a slam dunk case against me and it didn't help any that a few of my co-defendants had given written statements against me.

The lawyer let me keep the discovery so that I could go over it myself and he mentioned in the meantime he'd be trying to work with the State to try and get me a decent offer. He said he'd be back to pick the Discovery up because I had his only copy. This immediately raised a red flag for me. Why would my Attorney not have another copy of the Discovery of a case that was so high profile?

When I made it back to my housing unit I isolated myself from everybody by going in my cell and locking myself down. I wouldn't even get on the phone to call home. I went to work taking notes on over 700 pages of the discovery. The statements that I found inside devastated me!

On December 16, 2013 Mouth Peace had ratted me out for a Jr. bacon cheeseburger, a small fry, and a small soft drink from Wendy's, damn! Was that all I was worth to him? He could've at least asked for the Baconator. And then there were two guys from Houston that Flopp had picked up from the bus station that ratted too. But Flopp's statement bothered me the most because he showed no sympathy in his statement. I was hurt by his actions because he just knew entirely too much.

I also found out how I had been charged with the violent offenses. I had come to find out that one of my old cunning buddies named Lil' Black had made a statement against one of my street business partners named Ugh Moe. Lil' Black had stolen some pills out of some dude's car and sold them to Ugh Moe. Well, Ugh Moe found out that the pills were fake and he called me complaining about how he wanted his money back. I had already straightened out an incident before where Ugh Moe had accused Lil' Black of stealing two ounces of marijuana from him, and now I was putting myself smack-dab in the middle of another one.

I called Lil' Black and asked him to return Ugh Moe's money because the pills that he'd sold him were fake. He assured me that he would, but it never happened. He eventually started dodging Ugh Moe's phone calls.

So one day Ugh Moe had called me and told me he's had enough. He had come up with a plan to get Lil' Black over to his house and allow one of his homeboys to beat the shit out of him. Ugh Moe said that he would use his girlfriend to lure Lil' Black over to the house by telling him that Ugh Moe wasn't home because he was at the hospital having surgery on a bullet wound he'd suffered from earlier that year.

I agreed to be on the phone line listening in while the whole ordeal was taking place, not knowing that a wiretap had been placed on my phone. I will admit that I said some things that I'm not proud of. But I believe that if you live by the gun, then you'll die by the gun.

While I was reading about the ordeal in the Discovery I couldn't believe that the Detectives had heard a conversation about street justice being inflicted on an individual and they didn't intervene. They wanted to convict me on something so bad; they allowed this violence to play out in order to add additional charges on me, even through I had no direct role in what transpired.

To make matters even worse was the fact that Lil' Black actually had an outstanding warrant for his arrest at the time. So why would the Detectives allow a wanted man to remain free? What if Lil' Black had actually lost his life at Ugh Moe's house during the assault? Who is really more responsible for what happened, those who took an oath to protect and serve or me?

I further searched through my Discovery with a fine toothed comb and found out that Jack Frost had used the jails phones to get illegally recorded conversations with me. Usually inmates will use other inmates pin register numbers so they won't be identified while they are talking on the phone, in case there is some loose ends that need to be tied up on their case. But Jack Frost was calling me directly from his own pin number and even though we spoke in code, he was turning our conversations over to the Detectives.

Also, the money that was being used by Jack Frost's wife to buy contraband from me was the funding of the O.C.U. she would later claim, she was too afraid to testify against me because I was a high-ranking gang member. Bullshit! She wasn't scared when she allegedly purchased drugs from me!

Besides the incidents with Jack Frost and his wife there was no more physical evidence against me in the Discovery. Possession is nine-tenths of the law and all they had was a bunch of hearsay conversations. Unless the Feds were going to pickup the case, the State didn't really have me on anything. I couldn't really see the "slam-dunk" case that my lawyer was talking about, and I was going to show him all the flaws in the Discovery.

In the meantime I had to find some more cases that were similar to mine. I figured that the more I educated myself about wiretapping the more prepared I'd be in building up my defense. So I got on the phone and had my family to search the internet for any and everything concerning illegal wiretaps.

"Mr. Top Ten" eventually came back to the jail to retrieve the Discovery packet and asked me what I thought. I told him that all I'd seen was a bunch of B.S. and to me the case looked like a rush job. It seemed like the O.C.U. Detectives had added their own words to my simple phone conversations in order to make them illegal. The lawyer told me that he'd look over the Discovery packet again and get back with me in a couple of days. He also said the Prosecutor had an offer and wanted to know if I'd take it before my next court date.

A few weeks went by without me hearing anything from my Attorney. So I had my mother and my ex-girlfriend April's mother Patricia, go down to his office to pay him a visit. I wanted them to find out why he hadn't come to see me and let me know what the offer was from the State. He gave my family some arrogant spiel about how he was too busy to keep running over to the Jail to see me. He told them that although the State didn't have any real Physical evidence against me that I would still lose if I went to trail because I knew that I was a big drug dealer and that consequences came along with it. I couldn't believe that somebody whom I was paying would talk to my family like that.

He eventually made it over to the County Jail to visit me the day before we went to Court, and told me what the Prosecutors offer was. The State Prosecutor had it already set for me to sign for 19 years to run consecutive with my 6-year probation violation. He would drop everything if I agreed to cop-out to the 300 grams of cocaine, which is a Class A Felony and carries 15-25 years. I asked him if they really wanted me to do 25 years for some ghost drugs? On top of the fact that I didn't even sell cocaine was the fact that they'd only recorded allegedly 194 grams, and they didn't even have that evidence!

My attorney informed me that the Robbery they had against me was bogus, but that the State wanted to prosecute and convict me really bad. I wondered why the Prosecution would have so much dislike for somebody that they didn't know? I eventually fired "Mr. Top-Ten" and declined the Prosecutor's offer. And now that I'd found the State's angle I knew that I really had to focus on the wiretap application. I knew with the kind of hatred the Detectives had for me, they'd slipped up somewhere within the pages of the Affidavit.

18

Now It ALL Makes Sense

In the year of 2015, I further educated myself by attending Ashworth College in Norcross, Georgia. I received my Associate's Degree in Business Management. I'd always wanted to go to College but just could never find the time. My friend Big Baby found this program where people with a G.E.D. or High School Diploma could take classes via mail correspondence. Some people see this as a shortcut, but either way there are not a lot of people taking advantage of this wonderful opportunity.

I also became super knowledgeable about wiretap laws. I found exactly what I was looking for in the paperwork but I didn't expose my hand to my lawyers because I felt like they should already know. Plus, I had to stop trusting everyone, my Co-defendants, Lawyers, the State, and the Judge. I was told on multiple occasions that Judge Coffee had a personal vendetta against me. I figured that maybe he just didn't like Drug Dealers, period. But I found out later that the reason was actually more personal than what I'd thought.

After I fired "Mr. Top-Ten," I hired Attorney John Mobley from the Mobley Law Firm. Although he was a new Attorney, he had experience working with the Memphis Police Department for 11 years. From our first meeting I could tell that Mr. Mobley was inexperienced, but I really needed him to view my case from the eyes of a Police Officer, and he did.

157

Mr. Mobley reviewed the Discovery from the State and told me that it was a bogus cleanup job. But he also told me that he would step aside because he wasn't up to facing the kind of problems that came along with my cases. He agreed to give me a large portion of my money back and to refer me to an experienced Lawyer who would be willing to take the challenge with me. He said that he'd setup a Court date so he could go in front of the Honorable Judge Coffee and recuse himself and he'd bring my new lawyer along with him so that he could talk.

The court date was January 7, 2015, and on that date I sat down with the two Attorney's and made my claims: 1) I had reason to believe that my phones had been illegally wiretapped; 2) I had reason to believe that the prosecuting attorney, Paul Hagerman, had knowledge of the illegal interceptions of my phone calls and was intentionally involving himself in all of my cases because of a personal grudge or vendetta that he'd built up towards me. Based upon the fact that I'd filed complaints to the Internal Affairs about the un-professionalism of the O.C.U. Detectives in their investigations of me; 3) Paul Hagerman had only taken my case as a favor to the O.C.U. Detectives who were going through extreme measures to keep me behind bars.

I further explained to my two attorneys how I'd discovered that my phone was tapped before a legal wiretap order was secured. My co-defendant Terecka Wilson, a.k.a. Big Baby, had received two notification letters stating that her phone had been intercepted on two different occasions. One was from October 12, 2012 to March 13, 2013, and was signed by Judge Coffee. The other interception was on November 15, 2013 to December 16, 2013 and was involved in the case that I had pending in from of Judge Coffee. But, Judge Coffee didn't sign the second interception; Judge John Campbell was the one who signed it. So why would Judge Coffee preside over my case that stated my phone was only intercepted for 30 days when the evidence clearly showed that he signed a Wiretap Order for a previous 5 month investigation. An investigation , which more than likely involved one of my phones? If Big Baby's phone was tapped, then so was mine.

Neither letter received by Big Baby stated that she was the intended target of the wiretaps. Yet, she still ended up as my Co-defendant on the November 15, 2013 to December 16, 2013 wiretap interception. She wasn't charged in the previous 5-month wiretap signed by Judge Coffee. In fact, the Discovery packet had failed to mention anything at all about the 5-month Wiretap Investigation.

Both of my Attorneys listened to my theories and took down some notes. I told them that I thought it'd be a conflict of interest to allow Judge Coffee to preside over my case knowing that there were wiretaps he's signed that I still hadn't been notified about. My new attorney Paul Springfield agreed to take my challenging case and signed my court jacket that day.

Judge Coffee was very frustrated by the changing of my Lawyer for the third time. He told me that Attorney Springfield was stuck on my case and if I felt the need to change Attorneys again, then I could just represent myself. He set my court date for May 18, 2015, and I would later find out that Judge Coffee was more involved in my case than he'd actually let-on.

Mr. Springfield did a very thorough investigation on my behalf. He took it upon himself to make a trip to the Clifford Davis Building (Federal Building) to speak with the U.S. Attorneys Office. He found out they weren't interested in any of my current offenses. He also filed a "Motion to

Suppress the State's Evidence."

Mr. Springfield believed that the Detectives had mistakenly placed too much information in the affidavit. Like why would the State need to wiretap my phone when they clearly stated they had an informant (Jack Frost's wife) that personally made three separate drug purchases from me? And if that was true, then why didn't they make the arrest then? Their affidavit painted a picture of me as being "Mr. Untouchable." It read as if I was a hands-off kind of guy that employed my family and friends to do my dirty deeds for me.

Mr. Springfield also argued that there was a Discovery that the State hadn't turned over involving a separate Wiretap investigation that included my and was signed by Judge Coffee.

Under Tennessee Code Annotated (T.C.A.) 40-6-301: A wiretap application "stall" contain a "full" and complete statement of the facts containing "all previous applications" known to the individuals authorizing and making the application, made to any judge for authorization to intercept wire, or electronic communications involving any of the same persons, facilities, or places specified in the application, and the action taken by the judge on each application.

Judge Coffee pretended that he didn't know what was going on and gave the State the opportunity to explain. State Attorney Paul Hagerman responded and said that he'd spoken to the Detectives involved in the undisclosed 5-month wiretap and was told that it didn't involve me. They said the subject of that Wiretap was Big Baby's uncle J.T. who was under a separate investigation. After Judge Coffee had signed the wiretap and multiple extensions, it was only a coincidence that Big Baby's phone had been intercepted during calls to her uncle J.T. Yes and still, the State failed to mention this interception after Big Baby had been later indicted on my Wiretap investigation.

The State admitted having knowledge of me having and using multiple phones and that one or two of my phone calls may have been intercepted during their separate investigations. But in a later part of the transcript, the State contradicted itself by saying it didn't know if I'd utilized multiple phones or not.

Judge Coffee denied our Motion to Suppress. He said that one of his reasons was that he's spent the previous weekend before my actual trial looking through 8 years worth of boxes of affidavits that he's signed and the names in question didn't ring any bells for him. But, what struck us as strange was how when the State mentioned J.T.'s name Judge Coffee all of a sudden miraculously produced a file that involved J.T.'s case. That was a red flag for us because he had just stated that he reviewed 8 years worth of files in 2 days and saw nothing concerning J.T., or me or any of my Co-defendants so where did the file in front of him come from?

After our motion was denied, my Jury selection was supposed to begin at 1 p.m. Before that could happen my Attorney, Mr. Springfield, came back to the holding tank and told me that he's made the decision to withdraw himself from my case. He said that he would speak to the Judge and ask him if he could be recused. His reasoning was that he didn't want me to be forced into trial and he felt like my case had some "stinky fish." He said there was some much higher people involved in my case but he just couldn't tell me at the moment.

I was completely punch drunk hearing all of his from my lawyer on the day of my trial. I could have been bought for a dollar! Judge Coffee allowed the recusal. I remembered

161

him telling me that if I changed lawyers again that I would have to represent myself, but there he was, allowing me to change lawyers for the forth time.

Attorney Paul Springfield would admit later on that he had gotten a lot emails and phone calls from the State about my case and his involvement in representing me. Months later Mr. Springfield was disbarred from practicing law on a situation that I care not to discuss. My theory is that Judge Coffee and the State Attorney, Paul Hagerman, knew that he had raised some legitimate claims in my Motion to Suppress and they didn't want him to represent me to his full potential neither in my preliminary hearings or my trial.

Because Mr. Springfield had a conscience he couldn't live with himself for leaving me to be slaughtered. He spoke with a close friend of mine and told them that he'd refer me to an appropriate lawyer that didn't owe the State any person favors. He also said that he'd help my new lawyer from behind the scene for a more tactical representation.

I ended up hiring attorney Terrell Tooten who was hand picked by Mr. Springfield. After hearing my last two Attorneys' withdraw themselves from my case, and hearing how bad the State and the Judge had it out for me, I had doubts in my head about all of the Attorneys in Shelby County, in general. But I did cooperate with Mr. Tooten to the best of my ability.

Mr. Tooten had a lot of details about my case that he'd gotten from Mr. Springfield. But he told me that he wanted to do his own investigations and he's start by requesting another Discovery from the State and would match it up in comparison to the one he'd received from Mr. Springfield. He said that he would apply this method because he's seen occasions where the State had provided more or less discovery once a new Attorney had taken over a case. Once our motion for discovery had been filed then the State would have to go on the record saying that they had provided us with everything. That way if we felt like trial was necessary then the State couldn't surprise us with last minute evidence, without giving us a proper opportunity to prepare our defense.

In the meantime I continued to comb through the Discovery myself looking for any more clues showing that the Memphis Police Department Detectives did in fact illegally intercept my phone calls and text messages before obtaining a legal warrant. As faith should have it, one day while I was laying in my cell the C.O. delivered my newspaper (The Commercial Appeal) and right there on the front page was the words, "The Sting Ray Device" (Jones and Callahan, 2015) The article was about Police from all across the nation using several different methods to try to deter crime. There was a new system, however, that could monitor your every move and the Memphis Police may have been utilizing it.

The new system is an interception program called "Sting Ray" and it allows Law Enforcement to download nearby data. This data could be information stored on your phone or even a conversation that you are having right now. According to the Associated Press, at least 40 law enforcement agencies across the nation are using the String Ray device. The system itself can be moved around with ease and uses cellphone towers around it to operate. When the Memphis Police Department was asked whether or not they were using this technology, their spokesperson Karen Young said, "We are not at liberty to discuss how technology is used to enhance our ability to address crime."

The article practically blew my mind! There I was, accusing these Detectives of illegally intercepting my phone calls when the newspaper article came along and gave me the confirmation that I needed. Now, all I had to do was prove it.

19

ANOTHER Setback

That night I got down on my hands and knees and asked God to open up my mind and to reveal to me if the Officers had in-fact violated me. The bible says if you ask, you shall receive, and immediately afterward I felt a chill. And that whole night I read through my entire discovery from point A-Z and took notes. After exhausting all of my remedies I eventually found exactly what I was looking for, and it had been staring me right in the face the entire time.

On page 10 of the "Application/Affidavit" it stated, " On August 19, 2013, your affiant was provided a "Suspicious Activity Report Summary" from the Orion Federal Credit Union in Germantown, Tennessee where Kendrick Watson had previously opened an account and had taken out an auto loan in the amount of $31,672.73 for a 2008 Porsche Cayenne. The report begins by stating that every loan payment has been made in cash, and then describes one transaction in particular that occurred on August 19, 2013. The bank reported that on that day, Watson came into the bank and made the auto loan payment in cash. He then also deposited $100 in twenty dollar bills. Then, he removed from his pocket a very large stack of money held together with rubber bands. It contained $10,800 in twenties, tens, and five - dollar bills. He stated that he wanted one-hundred dollar bills in return. When Watson was informed that the bank would file a CTR on the transaction he altered the request and stated he only wanted $9,000 in the original $10,8000 to be involved in the transaction. Watson   then received 90 one-hundred dollar bills in return. This incident is "important" to your affiant not only because it demonstrates Watson's continued possession of large sums of cash and his suspicious activities with regards to that cash but also in your affiants experience, it is common for illegal narcotics traffickers who mail money to their supplier to use one-hundred dollar bills rather than smaller denominations. This allows for smaller, less suspicious and less detectable packages.

The next Court appearance, I showed Mr. Tooten my finding, and I told him to read the paragraph and tell me did he see anything suspicious. He told me he wasn't sure and asked me my opinion. I told him that I remembered the day quite well, I had got up that morning and gathered about $30,000 dollars in 5's, 10's, and 20's, I had did all this so I could either go to 3 different banks I had bank accounts with and change out 10,000 in each bank, something I normally did. I remember leaving my home and placed a call to Big Baby asking her could she meet me at the Orion Federal Credit Union in Germantown. She asked me why I told her that I would need her to help me change out at least one of the $10,000 dollar stacks, she told me she wouldn't be able to do it because she had to be at work that morning, so I was left along to take on the task myself.

Once I arrived at the bank, I actually did everything that the paragraph said I did, but my problem was how would a State Detective know what I did inside the bank if it was "Suspicious Activity" in a "Federal Bank" the exact same day of the alleged incident August 19, 2013, if he wasn't listening to my conversation with Big Baby that day. Because the way the Feds work, if I committed a Federal Act in a Federal Bank a State Detective wouldn't be the one to call, and they just skip over Federal protocol. To top it off why would they call the exact State Detective who's been investigating me. Either I'm stupid, or something is very fishy.

What Mr. Tooten said next sparked my interest. He said the he would personally go out to the Bank with subpoena in hand asking the Bank to give us a copy of the Suspicious Activity Report Summary (S.A.R.), Mr. Tooten than asked me did I see anything else in the Motion of Discovery that didn't seem right, I told him in fact it was. I believe this finding told me point blank that my phones had been intercepted illegally. I would go on to turn to pages 20 and 21 of the application/affidavit, and at the bottom of page 20 says:

A. Physical Surveillance

1. Your Affiant has performed physical surveillance on at least 30 separate occasions, and has observed Watson and his Associates to be very aware of law enforcement Actions. Watson has approached and acknowledged Surveillance cars on multiple occasions. Watson and his Associates have also been surveilled to employ counter-law enforcement tactics like "checking for tails," and informing others that they know the police are watching them.

In fact, continue on page 21, "Watson obtained the license plate number for Detective Acred and texted that number to several of his Associates so as to counteract surveillance.

These lists of reasoning are what Det. Johnathan Overly submitted to the honorable John Campbell on why he needed a wiretap on my phone November 15, 2013. I asked Mr. Tooten, "why would he need a wiretap?" If he already told Judge Campbell that I obtained Det. Acred, his partner's, tag number and texted it to my Associates as to counteract Surveillance. Why would the honorable Judge Campbell even sign the wiretap? If he actually read the Application/Affidavit like he should have.

I also informed my Attorney of the fact that I haven't

been to jail so it wouldn't be any reason the Detective should know what my text messages say while asking for a wiretap on my phone, plus, if they knew I actually sent out the text than I would need to now the dates, times, and the phone number I had at the time of the text. Mr. Tooten was in shock of my two critical findings all he could do is say the words I been wanting to here for a while "its over", but first we would have to figure out a way to box Judge Lee Coffee in because he's not gone let me embarrassed the State that easy.

So Mr. Tooten came up with a strategy. We would go on to have the Motion of Discovery Hearing and that he would also file a Motion to Disclose Hearing asking about the "Sting Ray" device. These motions were filed September 28, 2015. Mr. Tooten would also later on Email Prosecutor Paul Hagerman and asked him was the Sting Ray device used against me on my case? He knew we wouldn't get an honest answer I just wanted to confirm the fact the Memphis Police Department was in possession of such a power device that may very well violate the Constitutional Rights of every American citizen.

"The power of the "Sting Ray" doesn't only gather the data off the allege suspects phone, it all gathers the data of anyone in the suspects area that may or may not be using their cellular device no matter what phone company your with. The "Sting   Ray" a.k.a. "Cell Site Simulator," steals your phone frequency from your cell phone company's cellular towers at the time of its usage." (www.StringRay/HarrisCorporation.com)

The hearings for the motions to be heard were set on January 6, 2016. To our surprise, Mr. Tooten would prevail by hand delivering a subpoena to the Memphis Police Department Legal Division asking for all information about the "Sting Ray." I'm not gone enclose the woman's name but someone out of that Department slipped up and gave us the contract that was signed, at the time, by Memphis Mayor A.C. Wharton from The Harris Corporation spending large lump sums of cash on "Sting Ray" equipment.

On December 28, 2015 State Prosecutor would also respond back to Mr. Tooten's request asking about the "Sting Ray" device. This is the actual email:

"I forwarded your motion to Case Officers to try and see if they have anything you are asking for that I may not have. I don't think the attachments will help you but I don't think that you have them - the officers obtained ping orders (this is not   the Sting Ray device) for two of Kendrick's other phone at some point. These are two of his other phones (not the subject of the wiretap or that basis of any Application for a Wiretap) that were "pinged" at some point. "I also verified with them the "Sting Ray" device was never used on any of Kendrick's phones." And no other Wiretap Applications were ever filed on any of his phones either. I am sure the Officers have phone records for other people's phones during the investigation... if you want any of these, just tell me whose and we will see what they have.

In the email Mr. Hagerman never said that the Memphis Police Department was or was not in possession of the "Sting Ray" device.

On January 6, 2016, Mr. Hagerman would go on record and say that the State had given us all the Discovery. Judge Coffee would also go on record to say that all Discovery was completed. On January 12, 2016 at 3:55 p.m. Mr. Tooten was able to speak with the Orion Federal Credit Union Fraud Manager, Billy McCoy, after securing Mr. McCoy with a subpoena regarding the "Suspicious Activity Report" (SAR) in question. Mr. McCoy informed Defense Counsel that all

SARs would be submitted to him first, and then, if he deemed necessary he would then submit the SAR to FinCEN (Financial Crimes Enforcement Network). FinCEN is a part of the United States Department of Treasury. In addition, under the law, Mr. McCoy assured Defense Counsel that neither he, nor any employee from Orion Credit Union would, or could, provide SAR information to any Memphis Police Department Agent, because they are prohibited from disclosing the existence of an SAR, or any information that would reveal the existence of an SAR. In addition, no Memphis Police Department Agent (s) or detective (s) would be authorized to receive any SAR information. On January 19, 2016, Mr. McCoy then provided Defense Counsel with a letter explaining this. The letter states:

Dear Terrell Tooten,

In regards to your request for information relating to Suspicious Activity Reports that may or may not have been filed on Kendrick Watson, the Credit Union's response is as follows:

Banks are prohibited from disclosing SARs or even their existence. Furthermore, if a subpoena requests disclosure of a SAR or a SAR's evidence, the bank must decline the request citing the following code sections.

31 C.F.R § 1020.320 (e) (1) and
31 U.S.C § 5318 (g) (2) (A) (i)

~ Paul Hagerman

Mr. McCoy was basically stating that as powerful as a State Judge might be, they wouldn't be able to obtain this type of information without FinCEN approval.

My next court appearance was set for February 11, 2016;

trial was set on that day for September 12, 2016. My Attorney, Mr. Terrell Tooten, objected to having the trial date set since he was still in the process of receiving and going through Discovery. Judge Coffee wasn't trying to hear any of that. He was basically trying to force me into trial after my Attorney was telling him it was still crucial pieces of evidence out there that the State haven't provided even though the State went on record January 6, 2016 saying they have provided everything. Mr. Tooten would go ahead and file a "Motion to Suppress," on February 22, 2016. Arguing that the Wiretaps should be suppressed, based on different grounds that was previously argued by my last attorney, Mr. Paul Springfield. Judge Coffee would not let my Attorney set the "Motion to Suppress" for a "hearing," but instead, the "Motion of Suppress" was set for a "report date," so that my Attorney could argue the motion, and based on his argument, Judge Coffee would determine whether there "Motion" would be allowed to be set for a hearing. (Basically what Judge Coffee wanted me to do was give out my evidence I had against the State). The motion was set for May 31, 2016, as a Report Date, for Defense Counsel to make arguments regarding the motion. On May 31, 2016, Mr. Tooten alleged that he did not receive the entire Discovery requested from the State. Specifically, Defendant, when reviewing the Wiretap Application, concluded that the State could not have given him all Discovery based on information relating to: An alleged text message sent by Defendant; and an alleged Suspicious Activity Report (SAR) from defendant's bank. Judge Coffee than concluded that the State's Attorney Mr. Paul Hagerman was one of the most ethical Attorney's, and that Defense Counsel was being disrespectful and disingenuous, and attacked the State's Attorney's ethics when he represented that he had not gotten the entire Discovery. Judge Coffee than made a ruling for the record that all Discovery had been completed, and provided. Specifically here's what Judge Coffee said in the May 31, 2016 transcripts.

The Court stated, "What you've told the Court also is that you have not received a Suspicious Activity Report. We've Addressed Discovery. Mr. Tooten, Mr. Hagerman has told the court, has told you that he has given you – given all the counsel, Ms. Pasley, Mr. – Ms. McCluskey – absolutely everything that the State of Tennessee has in its possession."

(Transcripts from May 31, 2016 hearing, page 24, line 20 – page 25).

The Court then went on to inform Defense Counsel the following:

"I will not talk to you again, Mr. Tooten about Discovery. It is disrespectful to a Prosecutor who's sitting three feet from you, when you come to Court and you continue to say, "Discovery, discovery, discovery. Mr. Hagerman understands what his discovery obligations are, and I will again state for the record that he provides more Discovery than anybody else that I've dealt with. Whatever he has in his file, he'll provide it to you. If there's things that are discoverable, Mr. Hagerman understands, that discovery doesn't mean what he has in his file, what he has in his office, but any things that's in the possession of any agent of the State of Tennessee, Police Officers or otherwise. He understands that Discovery extends to folk that are Agents of the State, And it is disrespectful, and it is disingenuous when you come to Court and continue to yell 'Discovery,' continue to yell what you don't have and implying necessarily – necessarily saying that, 'Mr. Hagerman has things that he is not providing me.' And it is disingenuous and its disrespectful to continue to make those statements, and Mr. Hagerman is doing that he can to sit on his hands and not continue to jump up and down and say, 'I've given Mr. Tooten everything I don't have anything else.' I mean, he's flat out made the statement, 'I don't have anything else.' And you come to court and you continue to say' Discovery that I haven't got, 'and that's exactly, one hundred percent (100%), attacking the ethics of Mr. Paul Hagerman and you may say that, 'That's not what I'm doing, 'but that's exactly what you're doing Mr. Tooten, and I will not talk about Discovery anymore.

(Transcript from May 31, 2016 hearing page 41-42).

In that same hearing on May 31, 2016, my Defense Counsel then discussed whether filing a "Motion to Compel" would allow him to address the issue of missing Discovery again.

Specifically, Defense Counsel stated, "If I file a "Motion to Compel" based on documents that I need, will we be able to have a hearing on that?

Judge Coffee would cut my Attorney off by stating: Mr. Tooten, if you file a "Motion" in good faith that says, 'I believe this exists, and the State has refused to turn it over to me,' file it. But don't file a motion that you can't file in good faith.

Mr. Tooten: Well, Your Honor, everything –
Judge Coffee: Don't file – Mr. Tooten, don't file a motion that you cannot file in good faith."
(Transcript from May 31, 2016 hearing page 43-44)

That seemed to imply that the State had provided all Discovery to Defendant, and so, for Defense Counsel to then file a Motion to Compel, Requesting what he had been asking for, it would be a Request made in bad faith, and would be a personal attack on the State's ethical Prosecutor. Based on the arguments made by Mr. Tooten, Judge Coffee and the State had a clear understanding of what Defendant perceived to be problems with the State's wiretaps. Specifically, Defendant believed that the evidence clearly supported his position that the wiretaps were obtained illegally.

After addressing the Trial Court on May 31, 2016, I had my Attorney email the State's Attorney Paul Hagerman so we could continue building a paper trail on everything that's been going on so I could use at a later date. Defense Counsel reached out to the State regarding the State's WireTap Application, and the concerns that Defense Counsel had with it. The State, on June 7, 2016, then provided my Attorney with Suspicious Activity Report that was alleged to be addressed in the Wiretap Application. After receiving the Suspicious Activity Report (SAR) from the State on June 7, 2016, my Attorney, Terrell Tooten, and I were able to verify that the SAR was a complete fake.

The Detectives along with the State's Attorney had the nerve to provide me with something they made up and they used this information to get a Judge to grant them a "Request to Wiretap" my phone not to mention it's a Federal form. In relating to the text message I supposedly obtained one of the Detective's tag numbers and text it to my Associates as to counteract surveillance. Well on June 8, 2016, the State's Attorney Mr. Paul Hagerman admitted to my Attorney in person that the Detectives had lied saying, I sent out the text, but it was really my girlfriend at the time, LaRaye, who had actually sent out the text, now here's a second major lie, these Detectives basically didn't care what they submitted to the Judge rather the truth or a lie all they wanted to do in my opinion was cover up the fact they were already intercepting my phone calls illegally and they knew that the Judge who was taking the Wiretap Application/Affidavit would just sign the warrants without reading the information. (To this very day I have yet to see this allege text message, so basically the State's "ethical" Attorney has withheld this evidence from me). Mr. Hagerman had agreed to set up a meeting with my Attorney and Detectives Johnathan Overly and William Acred (a meeting that never happened). What I did have my Attorney do was, email each and every cancel or schedule meeting setting that he had with Mr. Hagerman. For some reason I knew Mr. Hagerman never wanted this meeting to happen. Here's full detail on how the emails went:

The meetings were initially scheduled to take place on either Monday, June 13, 2016, or Friday, June 17, 2016, but did not occur due to the unavailability of the witnesses. On June 24, 2016, it was communicated and clarified that one of the witnesses had been out of town, but would be back on the coming week. On July 5, 2016, the State informed Defense Counsel that they would not be available until July 15, 2016, and a proposed date of the following Tuesday was offered on July 19, 2016, Defense Counsel was informed by the State in person, that they are still working on setting up the meeting. The very next day July 20, 2016, my Attorney Terrell Tooten filed a "Motion for Continuance" asking Judge Coffee to allow Mr. Hagerman and himself an opportunity to conduct this meeting   involving key evidence, so that the matter can either be resolved or the issues   narrowed. Because I still had a trial date set for September 12, 2016, and they still haven't got the two Detectives responsible for the information relied on in the wiretap application to get a specific date. The "Motion of Continuance" was set for September 2, 2016, 10 days before my actual trial date, but in the meantime, Mr. Tooten on my behalf filed an "Amended Motion to Suppress and a Motion to Dismiss," on August 24, 2016, based on the information provided to us by the State. We knew with filing these two motions the State would be responsible on getting there own witnesses to court if Judge Coffee decided not to grant our Motion to Continuance.

In the September 2, 2016, "Motion of Continuance"

Hearing, Judge Coffee would pretend like he never knew that we had filed the two new motions, and when Mr. Tooten tried to inform him here's how that hearing went.

The statement, in part, of Defense Counsel went as follows:

"Based on the new evidence that I received, which I received after the hearing on May 31st [of 2016], in that hearing it was actually a finding made that the State had provided and completed Discovery. That was one of the issues we were   arguing about, is that I was arguing that there was some key evidence that the   Defendant did not receive. I believe the Court, based on the way my motions was written, interpreted those arguments to be speculative an conjectured and believed that I may have been disrespectful and disingenuous in arguing that the State had not provided everything, and that the Court got the impression that I was attacking the ethics, I believe, of Mr. Hagerman. So I tried to articulate on the record it had   nothing   to   do with him personally, it was based on what I was reviewing in my Discovery. And so on May 31st that conversation, rather passionately, ended with me agreeing that I would talk to Mr. Hagerman first and then see if we can resolve something, or address on any of these issues that I felt were still outstanding evidence. After that conversation in June, as I believe is spelled out in the "Motion of Continuance," I did in fact receive the additional evidence in which I was asking for."

(Transcript from September 2, 2016 hearing, page 10-11).

Judge Coffee responded in part, by stating that, "Mr. Tooten has indicated that he has additional motions to file because there may have been some things that might h a v e been done improperly, some things that might have been done wrong. And again, Mr. Tooten has indicated earlier, he's asking the Court to Speculate, and unless there is a legally sufficient written Motion to Suppress that is filed before this court, this court cannot and will not set a Motion to Suppress based on mere   speculation   or   conjecture."

(Transcript from September 2, 2016 hearing, page 29-30).

My attorney, did in fact have an amended Motion to Suppress filed, which was the based of defense Counsel's argument for the continuance, in order to allow the motion to be heard. When Defense Counsel realized that the Court was stating that the motion was not filed, he attempted to clarify, and the following exchange occurred,

"[Court names the basis of the Indictment That's the basis of this indictment that is set for trail on September 12th and the State of Tennessee, the alleged victims, also have alright to have a speedy trial on the case. And I will not delay this case any longer.

Yes, Sir?
Mr. Tooten: Okay, And I –
The Court: You interrupted me, Mr. Tooten.
Mr. Tooten: I'm sorry, I thought –
The Court: I thought you said, 'Yes, Sir.'
The Court: No, Sir. Don't – I said, 'Yes, Sir?" because you interrupted me.
Mr. Tooten: Okay. Understood. I apologize.
The Court: And I'm not going to argue with you today because I'm not going to let you spend my time, which you do every time when you come to court. I'm ruling. I would not entertain any, other arguments, and other statements."

(Transcript from September 2, 2016 hearing, page 34-35).

Therefore, Defense Counsel was never able to clarify on the record that an amended "Motion to Suppress" and "Motion to Dismiss"was filed on August 24, 2016. Even though Mr. Tooten went on Record and Clarified about missing Discovery, and that Detective Acred, a key witness for Defendant, on the Amended Motion to Suppress, as well as Defendant's Motion to Dismiss,was not available due to being on an indefinite sick leave.

(September 2, 2016 Transcript, page 7-8).

Judge Coffee still concluded in part, "I'm going to presume that Mr. Tooten had all of the information that Mr. Springfield [the prior Attorney Mr. Tooten took over the case from] had on this case. Mr. Tooten steps into Mr. Springfield's shoes. And Mr. Watson has deliberately has, has Deliberately, delayed this case for two and a half, almost three years...I'm finding for the record that this is simply a delay on the pact of Mr. Kendrick Watson that says, "I will delay this case Ad Nauseam.""

(Transcripts from September 2, 2016 hearing, Page 32-33).

Not to mention the fact, State's Attorney Mr. Paul Hagerman removed himself off the case and sent in a new Prosecutor, Mr. Austin Scofield, to attend the September 2, "Motion of Continuance" hearing. Mr. Scofield having no direct knowledge of the case went on record at the hearing acknowledged that there may have been misrepresentation in the Wiretap Application, but that the two issues presented by Defendant involved minute pieces of evidence. Mr. Tooten disagreed with the characterization of the evidence, and pointed to the fact that under the law, a hearing was necessary to resolve the legal issues presented. Judge Coffee would conclude the hearing by kicking my Lawyer out the Court Room, he knew I had the State in a jam and Judge Coffee did everything in his power to avoid me having those two crucial motions heard, but in part what my Defense Counsel did do on the day of September 2, 2016, after being kicked out of the Court Room by Judge Coffee, was he filed a "Application for Permission to Appeal under Rule 10 of The Tennessee Rules of Appellate Procedure" in the court of Criminal Appeals for the Western Division at Jackson Tennessee. This Appeal is basically an emergency Appeal when the Defendant feels that the Trial Court has stop outside of the guidelines of justice.

Mr. Tooten, argument went as follows:

Comes now Applicant, Kendrick Watson, and respectfully seeks this extraordinary appeal in order to allow applicant to have a "Motion to Suppress", and "Motion to Dismiss" heard prior to trial. Currently, the Trial Court will not allow applicant to have his motion heard, and this conduct departs so far from the accepted course of Judicial Proceedings, which requires immediate review from this Court. This appeal, if granted, would also help to provide a complete determination of this matter and may negate the need for an Appeal because if the Amended Motion to Suppress or Motion to Dismiss is granted, it would dispose of the case in its entirety. However, if these issues are not resolved before trial, Applicant would be severely prejudiced due to the delays involved in the standard appeal process and due to the costs that are accrued from having the matter heard at trial.

On September 9, 2016, the Appeal Court denied my Rule 10. In its denial it stated in part:

At the outset, we note that the application is lacking the requisite documents from which this court may make an informed determination concerning the Trial Court's actions on September 2, 2016. Furthermore, the Defendant's assertion that he has been denied a Pretrial Hearing on his renewed "Motion to Suppress" evidence and "Motion to Dismiss" is speculative given that the trial has not begun and the Trial Court may still conduct hearings on the matters.

(Rule 10 Order Denying Application)

I believe if I had the transcripts from the September 2, 2016 hearing showing Judge Coffee actions. I think I would have got a different ruling from the Appeals Court.

Based on the Order from the Court of Appeals, my Defense Counsel was prepared to ask for a "Motion" hearing right before trial, on September 12, 2016, however, on that day trial did not go forward due to the unavailability of Judge Coffee, (I be damned!). Judge Coffee did all this ranting about me delaying justice and I was the once holding up the process. Judge Coffee knew if he would have showed up the day of trial, he would have had to let me have my hearing on my two motions, (but little did I know Judge Coffee and State's Prosecutor Paul Hagerman made this case more personal than what I could imagine, it was a reason why Judge Coffee didn't show up for trial that day).

My court date was re-set for September 15, 2016 on that day judge Coffee would go on record apologizing to all party's for his absence and a new trial date was set for January 30, 2017. Also on doing that Court date of September 15, 2016, my Attorney, Mr. Terrell Tooten, would ask Judge Coffee for a hearing date so my two motions could be heard the conversation went as follows:

Mr. Tooten: Yes, sir. Your Honor, I would also ask if we could have a date set to be heard on our motions that we have filed. I spoke with Mr. Scofield with the State. I believe this is now his case. He text me back any day is good because he'll be here. I have a Motion to Dismiss and an Amended Motion to Suppress.

The Court: Has the State filed a response to those motions, Mr. Tooten?

Mr. Tooten: They have not filed a response.

The Court: I will not give you a motion date right now.

Mr. Tooten: Okay.

The Court: Talk to Mr. Scofield.

Mr. Tooten: Okay.

The Court: And have Mr. Scofield review these motions, and if Mr. Scofield tells me he does not need to file a reply to those motions, you and Mr. Scofield can address the court and we'll set it for motion date. But I don't set motions for hearings unless some parties, both parties tell me that they reviewed it, the state tells me they filed an answer, or tell me they don't believe that one is necessary.

(September 15, 2016, transcript pages 13-14).

Judge Coffee basically said that he'll set my hearing once the State gives him a written response or tell him if one was needed. On January 4, 2017 the matters were set for a hearing, and the State informed Judge Coffee that they were ready. However, the State failed to secure any witnesses, and anticipated making legal arguments only.

Defense Counsel did not bring any witnesses because he informed the Court that the State had the burden of proof, Id. The Court then went on to describe Defense Counsel's motion as a Motion to Reconsider. Id. At 7-8. The Court, in part, described it as a Motion to Reconsider, based on its position, "We presented the proof. We presented the Witnesses." Id. At page 27. However, Defense Counsel disputed that there was ever any witnesses called, and also went on to explain the new evidence he received with the

State's prosecution present, in order to assure the Court that there were no misrepresentations or differing views on the time line. Id. at 7-67. Specifically, Defense Counsel clarified that, "...my understanding   is that there has been no testimony taken on this matter at all, We've never had any witnesses testify under oath. Id. At 40. The matter was then reset to January 18, 2017.

(January 4, 2017 Transcript Page 7).

I'm sitting in front of my lawyer after the January 4, 2017 hearing like, can't you see this Judge is now trying to cleanup his screw-ups he realizing now that the State has a major problem I had you to present this information to him way back in your first "Motion to Suppress," on February 22, 2016, and he has took us through all these turns of events show he has the nerve to go on record and lie like we already had the hearing and the Detectives have already testified to my accusations. Judge Coffee abused his power as a Judge and tried to manipulate this system with his power by intervening on my Court Proceedings, and flat out lied for the State like we had this important hearing.

On January 18, 2017, the matter was set for 2 p.m. to be heard. When Defense Counsel appeared at that time, Judge Coffee disrespected him for being there at that time, based on a change in the Court's schedule that would have allowed the Court to allegedly hear the matter earlier. Defense Counsel was informed that attempts were made to reach him. Than Judge Coffee reprimanded my Attorney for making arguments about the case, when the hearing was starting at such a late hour. Than Judge Coffee went on record telling my Lawyer he went to the Appeals Courts and "lied" on him, but once I Request to purchase the January 18, 2017 transcripts Judge Coffee, personally held these transcripts for months and my Attorney and I notice that Judge Coffee had softened (meaning changed his wording) of what he actually said orally in court, I guess by now Judge Coffee has realized I was using his wording in all my court proceedings against him because he has been contradicting himself, for well over a year at that point. I personally felt that Judge Coffee has violated my Due Process, by allowing me to stay in Jail and him knowing those Wiretaps were granted illegally. But he refuses to give in and proceeded to try and help the State by abusing his power inside the Court Room. Here's the conclusion of the January 18, 2017 hearing between Defense Counsel and Judge Coffee.

Specifically, the conversation went as follows:

Mr. Tooten: Well, first argument and statement I would like to make is that I have never and on behalf of Mr. Kendrick Watson; we have never had a hearing in which witnesses were allowed to take the stand under oath and testify on this matter. So the fist thing I would want to argue and articulate is that we have yet to have a hearing where evidence and information was weighed under oath and subject to cross-examination.

Judge Coffee: Mr. Tooten, let's be careful with the Record because what you're saying Is also something that you alleged with the Court of Criminal Appeals, which is not true.

Mr. Tooten: What is that, Your Honor?

Judge Coffee: Which is that Mr. Watson has been denied a Suppression hearing. He has not been denied a hearing. He's had a hearing. Now, whether or not you were present and you conducted a hearing, that's another matter. But Mr. Watson has held, I provided Mr. Watson with a Suppression hearing. We've had that hearing. Testimony has been presented, witnesses have been called.

(January 18, 2017 Transcripts, Pages 9-10).

There was then a debate about whether I truly had a hearing in which witnesses were called with my Defense Counsel disagreeing that witnesses were never called, and disagreeing that he made false statement to the Criminal Court of Appeals when he made that representation.

Judge Coffee would go on to reset my next court date to January 26, 2017, four days before my schedule trial date in hopes of me finally having my two motions heard, boy was I wrong! When I made my court appearance on the 26 of January, My attorney, Mr. Terrell Tooten, had hit me with a devastating blow he told me that Judge Coffee had pulled him to the side off the record apologizing to not giving me my Suppression Hearing and that Judge Coffee has finally realized what I had been talking about the whole time, and if we would have been told him this, (I thought that's what my Defense Counsel and I had been trying to tell him since our first Suppression Motion that was filed February 22, 2016), he would have been resolved the matter, than Judge Coffee tells my Attorney that he got word I was about to be indicted on some additional charges and that I may want to look at what the State had as evidence to see if I would take a guilty plea on everything. "This is injustice at its finest!" How and the hell do the Judge know I'm about to be indicted one additional chargers? And what's it got to do with the issue that I have in his Court Room? I would ask Mr. Tooten.

Mr. Tooten replied he had no idea but we would have to see what the State had to present. Judge Coffee ended up agreeing to give me a Suppression Motion finally but he set it in July of 2017 and my new trial was set for November of 2017. On January 31, 2017, myself along with 17 others, were indicted for Conspiracy to Commit: Introduction of Contraband into Penal Facility;, Marijuana Conspiracy to Commit: Introduction of Contraband into Penal Facility; Cellphones Conspiracy to Commit: Money Laundering;

Introducing Contraband into a Penal Institution to Wit: Marijuana; Introducing Contraband into Penal Institution to Wit: ALPRAZOLAM; Introducing Contraband into a Penal Institution: Telecommunications Device (8 counts); Introducing Contraband into a Penal Institution to Wit: Marijuana; and Introducing Contraband into a Penal Institution to Wit: Marijuana Money Laundering. These new additional offenses blew my mind away! For one, I'm like how and the hell I let this happen and two, when I seen my sister Celitria Watson, long time friend, April Malone, and April's Mother, Patricia Malone, amongst the Names on the indictment. These are totally innocent people who hadn't done anything wrong but tried to support me and bring the mistreatment I was receiving in Judge Coffee's Court Room to the Public's Attention. All my Co-defendants where taken into custody or already in custody and eventually made bond. I was still puzzled to the kind of charges I was accused of because it's not such an offense as Conspiracy to Commit: Introductions of Contraband into a Penal Institution. I later found out that it was allegedly an investigation going on at the Shelby County Correctional Center a.k.a. The Workhouse (Penn form) that was named "Jail House Rock." This investigation was led by lead Detective Therman Richardson from the Memphis Police Department's Organize Crime Unit. I'm thinking to myself how much of a coincidence is this out of all people (Therman Richardson). I knew that something was fishy, but I couldn't panic I had to make sure all my friends and family was well taken care of first.

20

What's Next?

This was a under seal indictment so we skipped the general session stages and went straight to Criminal Court. Mr. Tooten had agreed to represent me no matter what the circumstances. The case ended up in Criminal Court Division 3 in front of the Honorable Judge Bobby Carter. I did my own background check on Judge Carter and I was told that he was one of them Judges that doesn't let cases linger around in his courtroom. Either you and the State work out a plea or he's setting you for trial. He likes to keep a clean docket. That was the good part, so I thought. I was also told that Judge Carter sides with the State if they're wrong or right. Judge Carter was once a Prosecutor in the Shelby County DA's Office along with Division 6 Criminal Court Judge John Campbell, and Division 7 Criminal Court Judge Lee V. Coffee.

Once I got arraigned and received a copy of the indictment, I looked it over with Mr. Tooten, I immediately let him know that this whole indictment was rigged up and a set-up, because I had know clue as to none of the charges against me, Mr. Tooten would then inform me that he had spoken with the State's Prosecutors leading the case Chris Scruggs and Austin Scofield and they told him that this was a new Wiretap Case and a guy, I'll simply call Theo, and myself were the Targets of the investigation. Come to find out Detective Therman Richardson claimed a Confidential Informant has been used in this investigation, but has been unable to identify all of the Co-conspirators, source of supply, and storage supply of illegal drugs. I didn't believe that for one minute but I had to listen to my Attorney explain to me what he knew all the way up to that point.

I admitted to Mr. Tooten while I was housed at the Shelby County Correctional Center on Maximum Security, I was utilizing a contraband cellular device and if the Wiretap were in fact true I had said a lot of cruel things about the State and Judge Coffee being corrupt, and that I couldn't see how I was allowed to have a cell phone in my cell and the outside police knew I had it and just let me keep the phone to find something else on me, because they knew their first case was a wrap. Mr. Tooten just stated to me let's just get the Motion of Discovery first and we could strategize from there. I told him no matter what the circumstances maybe I wanted to set this case for trial because for two reasons. 1. I knew my sister and I never discussed anything illegal on the phone, and 2. The 16-count indictment made no sense. We would eventually set my case for trial July 24, 2017 and Mr. Tooten promised to come out to the Pena form to visit me once he received the Motion of Discovery. The strange thing about all this, April Malone, my Co-defendant was accused of bringing contraband into the Pena form, but she was still able to visit me throughout the whole process. My sister, Celitria Watson, was pissed because she knew she didn't do anything wrong and she knew Detective Richardson had had a personal vendetta against me for years. April, her mom Patricia, and Celitria was falsely accused by Therman Richardson for having marijuana in there vehicles so they would have to pay to get there cars back at book value which cost more expense. They had to retain lawyers and make bond, the whole plain was to cripple my supporting cast and I retain a Public Defender, but Mr. Tooten wasn't letting that happen. Celitria and I had a conversation one day and she would say I bet you once we received our Motion of Discovery they gone been done fabricated my text message and if they do I'm gone break your case wide open and I'm thinking they might be stupid but it would be foolish to take it that personal to change somebody text messages. I told Celitria that I don't believe these Wiretaps are legal, I personally think they used the "Sting Ray" device because what logical Judge would sign a Wiretap on a contraband cellphone knowing I'm still going back and forth to court. I could be planning to physically hurt one of the staff members at the facility. I would later have my sister and April try to look up similar cases to mine and to know avail, "No results," either you introduce the contraband to a Penal Institution or you possessed it while in a Penal Institution.

Once we all retained our Defense Counsel the next thing was to wait, I still couldn't figure for the life of me, why would they indict us so quick and they didn't have the Motions of Discovery ready (I would soon get my answers). I could have resolved my issues in Judge Coffee Court Room and simply be fighting these second matters from the street. April would be the first to get a Motion of Discovery but here's the sad part, it wasn't her's, it was my sister, Celitria Watson's. April's Attorney, in which I refuse to give his/her name in credit in my journey, sent over my sister's personal information to April after telling her that she read my sister Motion of Discovery and listen to her conversation. I knew this was a strategy by the State, because they know I dealt with multiple woman and they know I would talk to my sister about anything. That method didn't work even though April and I had our choice words she remained loyal and kept our friendship intact. April would eventually give my sister her Motion of Discovery, I must admit my sister was pissed. Once my sister did review her Motion of Discovery (in which she never to this day got from her worthless Attorney), she did in fact discovery that her text messages had been altered and fabricated. The reason she knew this was because over the last 10 years every text message she had received or deleted was going to her Google account. Once she presented her findings to her Attorney he clamed that he would help her and he even admitted to her that State's Attorney, Paul Hagerman, was working both of my cases from behind the scenes and Austin Scofield was just the front guy.

He also told my sister that him, her attorney, and Paul Hagerman were close friends and that Mr. Hagerman had a personal vendetta against my sister and I because we had big mouths (That still doesn't give them the reason to falsify documents and take a innocent person into custody). My sister's Attorney agreed to let her speak with my Attorney if need be. Mr. Tooten would eventually come out to the Pena Form and visit me in early July, maybe two weeks before trial, he had finally received the entire Discovery from the State and I couldn't believe with my own eyes what he showed me.

On July 12, 2017 Detective Therman Richardson, Memphis Police Department, being duly sworn, depose and say as follows:Submitted Application and Affidavit for an Order Authorizing the Interception of Wire, Oral, and/or Electronic Communications, asking for my contraband phone to be intercepted and those Wiretaps was signed by "The Honorable Judge Lee V. Coffee."

I'm like what the hell, how could judge Coffee sign off on a warrant against me and I already got a pending similar matter in his court room, this Judge is breaking all type of laws, everything started becoming clear to me, Judge Coffee stalled me out for well over a year and was aiding the State and Memphis Police Department on fining other ways to entrap me even if it meant indicting innocent people. As Mr. Tooten and I comb through the Discovery, we noticed that Det. Johnathan Overly was aiding Det. Richardson in this investigation. Det. Overly was the leading Detective in my original Wiretap Investigation that I as trying to get on the witness stand for falsifying, and fabricating evidence, this is the same Detective that Judge Coffee would admit on numerous transcripts that had already testified to my accusations. I'm showing you corruption and injustice at its finest. Inside the Application/Affidavit would also point out to me that Detective Richardson copied and pasted certain parts of the Application because on page 15 it mentioned:

E. Search Warrants

33. The execution of search warrants in this investigation has been considered and it is the belief of your affiant that the use of warrants would not provide sufficient evidence to determine the full scope of the criminal conspiracy, the identity of all co-conspirators, and all of the locations at which drugs are stored. To date, Detectives believe they may have identified a location where warren PRATCHER conducts his cocaine transactions; however, Detectives are not certain that he used the same locations to store his supply of cocaine.

I'm like who is this guy? It was explained to me that Warren Pratcher, was another Target on a drug conspiracy case in the year of 2015, so why was this guy name in the place mines should have been remains the mystery question. Judge Coffee in my opinion never read this application, he just signed off on it, and I also verified that Judge Campbell also signed documents in the Absence of Judge Coffee. Judge Campbell still signs off on shady Wiretaps was all I was thinking. Mr. Tooten agreed that he would file a new "Motion to Suppress on Misconduct" for the Prosecution part because the State took Judge Coffee a new Wiretap Application/Affidavit and let him listen to my phone calls knowing my Defense Counsel and I was having problems with this Judge the entire time. Mr. Tooten also told me he would meet with my sister and review her evidence draw up a "Motion to Dismiss" due to the text messages being fabricated and he told me he would just ask Celitria's Attorney to join in on the

"Motion to Dismiss" that way her Lawyer wouldn't have to file anything.

These two motions would be filed in Division 3 in front of Judge Bobby Carter. My sister, April, and her mother would also set their cases for trial on the same day as mine, and Judge Carter assured everyone once trial was set all deals were off the table because he wanted this matter off his docket before the end of summer. I realized I had been trying to get some justice in Judge Coffee Court Room for three and half years but now I'm getting ready to go to trial on my second case less than six months. Once Mr. Tooten filed his two new latest matters everything changed. The State still wanted to try me, but file a Severance to separate my other three co-defendants, they no longer wanted to take them to trial, but they would be willing to dismiss their cases once I'm tried and convicted. After my sister's Attorney agreed to join in on my Motion to Dismiss for the fabricated text messages, he no longer wanted to do that, in fear of making the State mad and not dropping the charge against my sister (like she was guilty of a charge in the first place). Now all of a sudden Judge Carter had a change of heart after speaking so cocky on how all of us would be tried on the same day and it would be no deals after we all refused the States offer, now he was willing to grant the Severance with open arms. I would find out sometime later that Judge Campbell was actually Judge Carter's Supervisor when they were State Prosecutors in the DA's office in Shelby County. Mr. Tooten would finally get the opportunity to "Suppress" the second set of Wiretaps before The Honorable Judge Bobby Carter stating that the wiretap was not issued by a neutral and detached Judge. Specifically Defense Counsel Arguments went as follows:

1) As a general rule, a search warrant, or in this case, and authorization to allow a wiretap, should not issue unless its sworn before a neutral and detached magistrate or judge,

which establishes probably cause for its issuance. State v. Stevens, 989 S.W. 2d290, 293 (Tenn. 1999). In the present case, it cannot be said that the application for the wiretap was granted by a neutral and detached judge.

Defendant, and Defense Counsel, has had extensive interactions with Judge Coffee prior to, and during the time the State sought him to approve their Wiretap Application, regarding Defendant and his cases. The State sought a wiretap from Judge Coffee, while defendant's case was still pending before Judge Coffee, and while hearings were still being conducted. The changes in the case in Division III, as well as Division VII, are similar, and the State was providing Judge Coffee with information from Defendant alleged phone calls, designed to cause Judge Coffee to form a bias against Defendant. Judge Coffee received updates on Defendant on a regular basis, as it related to: Defendant's Division III cases; Defendant's VII cases; and updates that related to how he felt about Judge Coffee's courtroom, and his frustration with how he was being treated. By providing this information to Judge Coffee it only served to create a bias. Judge Coffee had reached negative conclusions regarding Defendant, specifically, that Defendant was attempting to delay his case, and essentially, interfere with the justice process. Defense Counsel has also had numerous interactions with Judge Coffee regarding Defendant, and the perceived illegality of the wiretap. The State, knowing that there were challenges made to Judge Coffee regarding his discovery was handled and how the wiretaps were handled, took it upon itself to seek new wiretaps from Judge Coffee, against Defendant, giving the appearance that they were trying to go to a Judge who they knew had an image of defendant that was not favorable, and they went during a time that they were aware of what had transpired between Defendant, Defense Counsel, and Judge Coffee. There has been no explanation, to this date, as to what gave the State the impression that they were before a neutral and detached judge, as it related to defendant, and the procuring of the wiretaps. Also, the State Appears to make a conscious effort not to clearly articulate, any where, on any of its request for wiretaps or pen and trace evidence, that Defendant had a similar case before the same judge in which they were seeking the new authorizations. There is no justifiable reason to omit this information.

B) The State made knowingly False Representation To Secure The Wiretap

Fourth Amendment violations are addressed in part, by the exclusion of evidence, under the Exclusionary Rule. "The rule thus operates as a judicially created remedy designed to safeguard Fourth Amendment rights generally through its deterrent effect, rather than a personal constitutional right of the party aggrieved." '[citation omitted] U.S. v. Leon, 468 U.S. 897, 906 (1984). "First the exclusionary rule is designed to deter police misconduct, rather than to punish errors of judges and magistrates," Id. At 916." Suppression therefore remains an appropriate remedy if the magistrate or judge issuing a warrant was misled by information in and affidavit that the affiant knew was false or would have known was false except for his reckless disregard of the truth." [citation omitted] Id. At 923. In this case the State recklessly disregarded the truth when it represented, under oath, when relating to whether there was any previous applications for wiretaps against Defendant, stated that it did not have knowledge of any previous applications made to any circuit or criminal Judge of the Thirtieth Judicial District authorizing to intercept communications involving the target facilities that are subject of this previously been indicted for their involvement in a conspiracy to distribute marijuana in an amount greater than 300 pounds. This previous investigation involved the use of Court ordered interception of wire, oral, and electronic interception. The previous investigation occurred in late 2013 and culminated with the drug trafficking organization bring indicted in February of 2014." In fact, the situation was far more volatile. For one, the previous case involving the wiretap is not only still pending, but still pending before the same Judge who the State was seeking a new wiretap application from. Also, the timing on the request is suspicious, in that it was requested, while the previous wiretap issues were being challenged, with arguments being made t suppress the evidence obtained from it. None of that information is contained in the State's phrasing of the previous investigations involving the wiretap. Under T.C.A. 40-6-304 A wiretap application "shall" contain a "full and complete statement of the facts containing all previous applications known to the individuals authorizing and making the application, made to any judge for authorization to intercept wire, oral or electronic communications involving any of the same persons, facilities, or places specified in the application, and the action taken by the judge on each application; and where the application is for the extension of an order, a statement setting forth the results thus far obtained from the interception, or a reasonable explanation of the failure to obtain results." This was not done in this case, as required by law. Amy Weirich, the District Attorney, in her written authorization for the wiretap application, dated July 6, 2016, and the extension, dated August 12, 2016, clearly stated that she had no knowledge of any previous wiretap applications and never referenced the previous application made in 2013. Therefore, it is very concerning as to why this information was not clarified, or corrected, if it were false. The proper assumption would be to conclude that her written, signed representations were true, and that she was not aware of the previous wiretap application of defendant, and this the wiretap order was not secured legally. The applicant, in his application, even incorporated the authorization from Amy Weirich by reference. Defendant contends that in his present cases, a wiretap was obtained against him based on illegal wiretaps, illegal evidence, false representations to the court, or the by-product of illegal evidence.

In addition, defendant contends that any and all orders allowing for any form of   wiretaps, electronic, or any other form of surveillance, was based upon insufficient application for a wiretap, insufficient information, and therefore, any and all evidence obtained must be suppressed. In the typical "fruit of the poisonous tree" case, the questions before the court is whether the evidence obtained against the defendant was obtained by illegal means, and it so, whether there have been some intervening circumstances sufficient enough so as to remove the "taint" imposed upon the evidence, based on the original illegality.

United States v. Crews, 445 US 463, 471 (1980). In the present cases, the State and the Memphis Police Department used illegal evidence, misrepresentations, and illegal wiretaps, in order to attempt to obtain a legal wiretap. Due to this conduct, the evidence has become "tainted," making any use of the evidence the fruit of a poisonous tree. Specifically, Defendant's communications have been unlawfully intercepted, and therefore, the evidence should be suppressed under T.C.A. 40-6-304 (h) (1). At best, in the light most positive to the State, and ignoring any negative inferences whatsoever, there could be an attempt to argue that the conflicting language involving the District Attorney, in comparison with the rest of the application, was a misstatement, or that there is just an ambiguity. However, in the case of an ambiguity, any and all ambiguity "shall" be resolved in favor of the aggrieved party and against the State. T.C.A., 40-6-310. Therefore, any potential ambiguity surroundings any of the issues presented should be resolved in Defendant's favor, and against the State.

C) The State failed to provide a full and complete Statement

The State's Wiretap Application fails to comply with the T.C.A 40-6-304 (A) (2), which requires that the application provide a "full" and "complete" statement of the facts and circumstances in which reliance is placed upon, in order to justify the applicant's belief that an order be issued. In this case, the State makes references to Warren Pratcher, a party who is not listed as a target to locate where Mr. Pratcher keeps his cocaine, but has failed to provide Defendant with any information on Mr. Pratcher, or any context supporting its assertions. The State, instead, produces an incomplete statement, as opposed to a full and complete statement, as required by law. In addition, the application includes information that details that Defendant, and alleged associates of Defendant's had their phones monitored between the time periods of May 23, 2016, until June 22, 2016. However, there was never a request made for a pen trace and register of Defendant's phone until June 30, 2016. There is no explanation offered or no full and complete statement given as to how that was legally possible. In the application, it also named several co-defendants of defendant, to his Division Vii cases, yet the application failed to inform the court that the individuals were co-defendants, and that at least one of the individuals Ronald Hudson, was currently set before Judge Coffee, with an active case that was the basis of the previous wiretap an active case that was the basis of the previous wiretap issued in 2013.

Judge Bobby Carter would give the State the opportunity to make there argument, the State's Attorney Austin Scofield failed to State any legal grounds on how was I able to obtain a contraband cell phone while in custody, and the Judge and Police had knowledge of the fact but maintain to let me utilize the device, all the State's Prosecutor could say was that I shouldn't have had the phone in the first place, that may have been true I shouldn't have had the phone but does that give the Memphis Police Department the right to alter and fabricate the text messages of innocent people because they wanted me off the streets that bad, Judge Carter would go on to deny the Suppression motion but with no legal ground, but stated he would let the Appeals Courts make a decision on whether or not it was legal to secure a wiretap warrant on a contraband cell phone and if I had right to privacy. I eventually entered a guilty plea and was sentence to over 49 years some offenses to be ran concurrent and some consecutive. My sister and April's charges were later dismissed and they waited for a while and recuperated and they both filed federally lawsuits. ~ I.C.E.

21

When Will Someone Listen?

Cruel and unusual punishment penetrates the grounds of Morgan County Prison. It resides within the Staff. How long do we have to endure the life of an animal? Morgan County Prison is located in Wartburg, TN. This prison has one of the nastiest kitchens in the state of Tennessee. The kitchen is infested with roaches and rats. Trays are continuely being wet. Food is half cooked and portions are not what they are supposed to be. There have been several cases of food poisoning.

Teachers are not teaching inmates in GED or Vocational Classes. Majority of the times teachers aren't even present, but yet and still, inmates are forced to sit in classes or in some cases report to the Education Building, that's an automatic disciplinary write. All have write-ups have strong possibilities of effecting your chances of a eligible parole release day. Inmates sit in those classes for HOURS not learning ANYTHING. The Prison System continues to receive grant money for programs. These programs are suppose to help rehabiliate inmates. Commissary is suppose to be a privilege, but yet and still, the commissary price triples the average salary for an inmate, 17 cents an hour. Basically, inmates are laboring for free within the prison walls. The State takes all or half of State draw, due to court costs and fines.

The Officers extort inmates. They bring in the drugs and cell phones, and they'll use one of the Officers on another shift to come take away the contraband and charge you money to not write you up. Then they'll resell the contraband to other inmates across the Prison. There have been numerous cases of this at Morgan County Prison were inmates have been beaten to death. When will some one listen to the cries within these walls? Truth is we are labeled as Criminals, a mistake was made in our lives. Law-abiding Citizens do not understand what is going on within these walls. The government gives this picture perfect painted image for the American public that's not realistic.

Prison is suppose to be a Rehabilitation Center for Criminals. Inmates are not getting rehabilitated in the Prison System. Prison is one of the number one businesses in America. We're being auctioned off every time some one goes before a Judge. It's about housing as many inmates as possible. Some are wrongfully convicted or over sentenced. Americans pay taxes. More prisons are being built, Tax Payers believe Justice is being due according to the law. That's not true! When you're on the outside looking in, the Judge, DA's Office, along with the Police, manipulate the law. In some instances a lawyer will convince the ignorance or lack of knowledge of their client to cop out of a deal to receive a conviction knowing their case has Constitutional Violations.

Just about everyone is aware of the injustice within the Criminal System. When will change come? When will the Prison System get addressed for her actions? Her skirt has been raised for decades to a society of men and women who get taken away from their families. Where is the money from grants and tax payers really going? Wardens of Prisons work together with Staff to dress up the issue. Tennessee Department of Corrections (TDOC), Head Quarters is located in Nashville, TN. Nashville is aware of the problem, Nashville is not fooled during yearly inspections. Why hasn't Nashville put forth an effort to address the prison issues? It's a business.

Epilogue

Eye See Everything that's happened to me throughout my life. As a child growing up, even though I may have seen the situation before hand, regardless if it was right or wrong, I still chose to involve myself. I dreaded for a long time about writing my Testimony but the Great Dr. Martin Luther King once said, "The ultimate measure of a man is not where he stands in moments of comfort and convenience, but where he stands at times of challenge and controversy."

I can admit I was worried about what people would think, but as time went on, some of God' greatest Saints spoke to me, and prophesized that I had a strong message to deliver through my own life experiences. I was told don't sugar coat, let it all out, and confess my sins to not only God, because He has forgiven me, but to the world. Be honest and open minded towards myself, I made the choices I made not only to correct them, but also to make an impact on other people's lives. As you could see, I got off my knees from a long prayer, picked up my pen and pad, and took you on a journey. A journey of a young boy who was lost, despite his age of 18 making him legally an adult; a young boy who still wasn't sure of how to be a man. The enemy controlled his well being and his since of direction, and just about guided him into eternal self-destruction.

As I wrote, I let my heart do the talking for me, and I began to shed away the guilt I had placed on myself for being a wicked human being. I blamed society for my mother's drug use. I even looked to blame some one for my own negative endeavors, but as I look in the mirror at the person I strive to be, I rehab my mind to take life one day at a time. I hear a lot of time on how the United States is divided by racism, to be honest who cares; look at how far we've come. People are only divided by their selfish hate and use skin color as an excuse to do just like I did, blame society.

For a while I was totally pissed at the Justice System over the type of hand I was dealt, but I can't blame anyone but the man in the mirror, myself. If I would have taken a productive path, I probably would have got way better results. Dr. King once said "We need leaders not in love with money, but in love with justice. Not in love with publicity, but in love with humanity." I wouldn't have put myself in a position to even characterize the injustice of the legal system. Those within the legal system, who I encountered, also would have no opinion of me, if I weren't doing illegal activity. I close my testimony with the message that "no weapon formed against me shall prosper."

Sincerely,

I.C.E

Appendix

Court Proceedings
Documents & Transcripts

Mid South Peace and Justice System

Re: Criminal Justice in Memphis Tennessee

Many of us are concerned about how the Shelby County District Attorney General continues to get a way with all the Civil Rights Violations? Maybe her license to practice law should be revoked.

What do you think? You should really check out this unusual criminal justice system which fosters disregard for constitutional rights such as, among others fast and speedy trials; and the utilization of fabricated information to bold pretrial detainees in an already overcrowded jail in order to obtain coerced guilty plea bargained convictions. An important question pertaining to many cases should be asked! "How can the prosecution not know that the reported allegations against a person supporting the offense are fabricated?" It would seem like the Shelby County District Attorney General, Amy Weirich, would have competent process to review, and screen out, cases which have insufficient, or questionable, evidence because the overall process is fundamentally flawed. The following cases are brief examples of the magnitude of abuse within this unusual system.

In <u>State v. Noura Jackson</u> (2014) WL4161966, the

DA withheld exculpatory evidence. The during trial made inflammatory comments on Jackson's fifth amendment privileges; and the introduction of the inadmissible bad act evidence was overwhelming. However, the Supreme Court reversed and remanded with strict instructions to the trial court.

In <u>State v. Vern Braswell</u>. A hearing began in trial court on or about November 21, 2014 regarding an envelope that was found and marked: "Do not show defense," signed by the DA's initials. The Prosecutor who was responsible for (finding it) was transferred to another division. And now the envelope s=disappeared from the case file.

In <u>State v. Johnny Ingle</u>, #13134884. After being forced sat in jail for over a year on a "Bogus aggravated burglary offense, on September 23, 2014, the DA dismissed the case, and Mr. Ingle was released. Although there was not a single piece of credible evidence connecting Mr. Ingle to the alleged burglary. The magistrate who presided over the preliminary hearing bound the case over to the grand jury, and clearly in order to obtain the True Bill, the prosecutor had to have presented false and misleading information to the grand jurors. Additionally, Mr. Ingle's defense Attorney advised Mr. Ingle tat he would receive a 10 to 15 years prison sentence if he rejected the DA's 6ix year guilty please offer. The question n this case is how could the DA have not known that there was not evidence in which to convict Mr. Ingle, but kept him in jail for over a year? And this case is no any isolated incident. The difference between Mr. Ingle and many others similar cased is that most accept a coerced guilty pleas bargained conviction whereas, Mr. Ingle held out, and ran the risk of being forced to trial on false and misleading information which Amy Weirich should have known to be false. Furthermore the habeas Petitioner, carl Neal, filed a 42 U-S-C 1983 lawsuit inn U.S. District Court (sec <u>Neal v. MPD</u>, et al — No.2:14-CV-02851-JOJ-tmp), alleging false arrest and of course, the civil suit has "other allegations" that are not contained in the habeas petition, which highlights the extraordinary disregard for trustworthy information. Habeas Corpus petition may be necessary to fully understand the significance of the DA's disregard for having reasonable trustworthy information for believing that a person is guilty. The "other allegations" are fully supported by documentary evidence not surprising, however, is that the DA's office is the agency that compiled the documents, and provided them to Mr. Neal's criminal defense attorney and therefore the DA has first hand knowledge of the documents content for the record, the preliminary hearing record in <u>State v. Neal</u>, No. 13-05402, has up and simply disappeared. The trial court judge ordered a new preliminary hearing, and would not entertain the application for writ of habeas Corpus. These cases cited are examples of the widespread, deeply-rooted abuse. The DA has violated, why is this? Although the constitution provides for speedy trials, the DA, together with Criminal Court Judges are systematically depriving the majority of pretrial detainees of their (this) right. The abuse goes on and on. There it is a preview on how the American Justice System works in Memphis, simply Incredible.

****

To access Kendrick Watson's transcripts go to:
https://www.dropbox.com/sh/awu4d6e88huy8ea/AAC-iiojHakQUT9hL8Fetoefa?dl=0

About the Author

Kendrick Dejuan Watson is an entrepreneur, son, brother, uncle, cousin, and friend. Born in Mabayou, Mississippi, affectionately known as Jerry to family and close friends, he is no stranger to life and the ups and downs that come with it. Going against the grain and not afraid to challenge the validity of any situation, Kendrick has always been a straight shooter.

With "I.C.E.: Eye See Everything - The True Life of Kendrick Watson (All Facts ~ No Fiction), Kendrick wants everyone to know about his life experience as well as the injustice in our, so call, legal system.

"If you're going through any legal procedure make sure that you look into your case thoroughly. The problem is the people that we have governed over our lives are not always as ethical as they should be. Some of them make decisions off of their personal feelings toward the individual."

Kendrick wants to leave a legacy that will help and inspire others who are dealing with the same or a similar situation as him. Mr. Watson believes "sometimes it's better to speak out and release your pain and frustration out on paper than taking physical action towards another person" and "I.C.E." was the perfect way for it to do just that.

Mr. Watson is currently serving a 23-year prison sentence at Morgan County Correctional Facility in Wartburg, TN. Kendrick is the father of Torey, Kendarius, Corey, Traven, Demario, Acasia, and Kourtland.

Education; Trezevant High School (1998) F.C.I of Memphis Federal Prison GED (2000) Ashworth College Associate Degree in Business (2015)

Coming Soon...